AYAGOGY: AYAHUASCA AS A SOCIAL CHANGE AGENT AND LEARNING MODEL

ROAN KAUFMAN

Inner Dimensional Media
515 Cedar Street
Madison, WI 53715

More information: ayagogy.com
To contact Roan Kaufman directly: rkaufman@email.fielding.edu

Copyright (C) 2016 Roan Kaufman

All rights reserved. This book, or parts thereof, may not be reproduced in any form without permission. The scanning, uploading, and distribution of this book via the Internet or via any other means without permission of the publisher is illegal and punishable by law. Your support of the author's rights is appreciated.

Printed in the United States of America
10 9 8 7 6 5 4 3 2 1

Inner Dimensional Media ISBN-978-0-9970075-0-3

Library of Congress Cataloging-in-Publication Data has cataloged the following edition:

Kaufman, Roan.
Ayagogy: Ayahuasca as a Social Change Agent and Learning Model / Roan Kaufman. —1st ed.
p. cm.
Includes bibliographical references.
ISBN-978-0-9970075-0-3
1. Education 2. Adult Learning 3. Ayahuasca 4. Psychedelic studies

To my father, Jack Kaufman
1939-2013

TABLE OF CONTENTS

INTRODUCTION — 1
    Background — 3
    What is ayagogy? — 4
    A call to action — 7

CHAPTER 1: OVERVIEW — 11
    Contextualizing the problem — 11
        Personal statement — 14
        Indigenous knowledge — 19
        About ayahuasca and ayahuasca ceremonies — 20
        Limitations and challenges in the research — 26

CHAPTER 2: HEGEMONY, WESTERN HEGEMONY, AND COLONIZATION DEFINED — 29
    Hegemony defined — 29
    Western hegemony — 33
    Colonization — 37

CHAPTER 3: PRESENTATION OF THE RESEARCH INTERVIEWS AND QUESTIONNAIRE COMMENTS — 39
    Data from interviews — 40
    Excerpts from interviews with anonymous ceremony leader — 47
    Qualitative scaled questionnaire comments — 52

CHAPTER 4: THE FIVE ANTIDOTES TO WESTERN HEGEMONY CONNECTED TO WORKING WITH AYAHUASCA   61

    Antidote 1: Movement from the personal trappings of Western hegemony towards self-determination   65

    Antidote 2: Movement from individuality and "survival of the fittest" towards relationality and a kinship-focused orientation   72

    Interview with Sobonfu Some on relationality and community   83

    Antidote 3: Movement from anthropocentrism towards viewing the natural as World as Sentient   92

    Antidote 4: Movement from valuing materialism and consumerism towards meaning and purpose beyond these structures   101

    Antidote 5: Movement from acceptance of Western hegemonic institutions towards criticality or rejection   108

    Interview with Michael Yellowbird on Indigenous views of criticality   109

    The Indigenous worldview versus the Western worldview   124

CHAPTER 5: INTERVIEWS WITH EXPERTS: RICK STRASSMAN, ALAN SHOEMAKER, RAK RAZAM   128

    Rick Strassman   128
    Alan Shoemaker   134
    Rak Razam   138

CHAPTER 6: PROBLEMS WITH AYAHUASCA USAGE IN THE WEST AND BY WESTERNERS   145

    Ayahuasca Cannot Be Understood   146
    Cultural appropriation   149
    The influences of Christian hegemony on legality and illegality   153
    Commodification   145
    Abuse of power by ayahuasca leaders   158
    Psychonauts   161
    Lack of post-ceremony social support   163

CONCLUSION   167

REFERENCES   171

Acknowledgements

I have so much gratitude to so many people who were instrumental in the creation, research, and publication of this book. Much gratitude to my mentor in my doctoral program at Fielding Graduate University, for his encouragement, inspiration. Four Arrows has taught me so much about Indigenous cosmologies, hegemony, and mentored me to become a scholar practitioner dedicated to social change.

Thank you to those who have offered encouragement and assistance with my research and editorial process: Martha McCamy, Amy Gile, and Marcelle Richards. Thank you all for your help in clarifying my vision for this book and making my writing approachable. Thank you for your help in completing my doctoral dissertation. Thank you also to my dissertation committee: Dr. Rena Palloff, Dr. Kathy Tiner, Dr. Connie Krosney, and Christina Lewis.

Much gratitude and appreciation to the following people for their input and dialogue regarding the themes in this book: Paul Beck, Bill Hamilton, David Schinke, Alan Shoemaker, Tony Beck, Chris Olson, and Nicole Eby.

Great appreciation to Tatiana Katara for the incredible cover art and Holly Henschen for layout and design.

Thank you to my family: my father Jack Kaufman, who encouraged me to start the doctoral process and was my biggest academic champion until his passing in 2013, my mother, Dorothy Helman, my sisters, Erica Heisman and Jill Heisman, for their strong support. Thank you to Myron Eshowky for being a strong advocate, teacher, and friend, and for your support and encouragement in following my passionate interest in ayahuasca.

Thank you to everyone who helped me raise funds for the publication of this book via Kickstarter including:

Amy Chaffee, David Ornstein, Dmitri Bilgere, Katharina Mark, Erica Heisman, Mia Morrisette, LaDona Wheatley, Brendan Connelly, Shawn Streepy, Marcelle Richards, Mike Dalcher, Deborah Darby, Sue Helman, Craig Pomatto, Constance Juday, Craig Pomatto, Rebecca Welty, Laura Zirngibl, Rob Summerbell, Robert Waterman, Matt Felgus, Erik Nordtvedt, Neil Smith, Joel Burbach, Brandon Norsted, Craig Hall, Karen Lasker, Kristy Kette, Laurie Geving, Suzy Kathleen, Lauren Hambrook, Chris Olson, and Barry.

Thank you to the people who were interview subjects for my research and to those who were interviewed for this book

Thank you to the courageous people around the world who work selflessly with plant medicines to heal and teach and bring people back to harmony with themselves and this world.

Introduction

> *Ayahuasca brings us to the boundaries not only of science,*
> *but also of the entire Western world-view and its philosophies.*
> (Shanon, 2002, p. 39)

Ayagogy: Ayahuasca as a Social Change Agent and Adult Learning Model, is based on the ayahuasca mixed methods research study I conducted for my doctoral dissertation, as part of the requirements for my doctorate degree in Educational Leadership for Change (EdD) from Fielding Graduate University. I have edited and revised the dissertation to be livelier and readable and to more clearly address the issue of how ayahuasca can be a social change agent and a model for adult learning. I have also included interviews with a few experts in the field of entheogen and ayahuasca studies, so that the discussion of ayahuasca would be more well-rounded and represent differing viewpoints. I have included sections from my interviews with DMT and ayahuasca experts Rick Strassman, Alan Shoemaker, Rak Razam. I have also included parts of my interview with Indigenous scholar Michael Yellowbird to contribute to the exploration of Indigenous wisdom. It is a tremendous honor to also include an interview with one of the foremost voices in African spirituality, Sobonfu Some, who spoke to me about Indigenous notions of relationality and the role of community within a healing context.

When I began to clearly see how destructive Western hegemony is to the people and sentient beings of our planet and the natural world, and the covert, manipulative and ubiquitous quality of hegemony, I wondered why others researching or even discussing plant medicines and plant teachers were not including this type of social critique infused into their research. Issues about hegemony began to haunt me. How have we moved so far away from being in a harmonious relationship with the natural world and other human beings? How did the destructive forces and beliefs of materialism and commodification become so deeply infused in my own belief systemes and even my worldview? I found myself passionate about researching and exploring this untapped combination of the wisdom of plant medicine ceremonies, such as ayahuasca and its grounding within Indigenous wisdom, with the power of the human spirit and heart to overcome oppressive forces in any form. The ayahuasca experience may be able to both highlight some of the invisible forces of hegemony and oppression, while at the same time helping individuals heal themselves, thus it is a powerful force to investigate. It is my intention that this book serve to open up new avenues of dialogue regarding the potential plant medicines hold to heal not only individuals, but to reach globally to free our world from the enslavement of hegemonic infleunces.

Background

The fields of ayahuasca and psychedelic studies tend to paint a picture of plant medicines as primarily used to help individuals heal on physical and emotional levels, to understand themselves at a deeper level, and to assist in helping individuals change their personal lives. Missing from much of the ayahuasca literature is the contextualization of ayahuasca as a potential agent of social and political change, and a possible vehicle to bring about hegemonic awareness.

For example, Winkelman (2005, 2014) and Winkelman and Roberts (2007) have researched the potential ayahuasca has to help drug addicts overcome addictions. The psychotherapeutic along with some of the potential medical uses of ayahuasca have also been explored (Barbosa, Cazorla, Giglio, & Strassman, 2009; Bouso & Riba, 2014; De Rios, 1984, 1996; Frecska, White, & Luna, 2003; Labate & Cavnar, 2013; Topping, 1998; Tupper, 2002, 2008 2009a, 2009b). Researching the medical and psychotherapeutic potential of ayahuasca, and attempting to legalize hallucinogens as potential healing remedies, is noble work. This focus, however, is not the same as researching the social change aspects of hallucinogens, plant medicines, or ayahuasca, which is the focus of my exploration. Furthermore, researching ayahuasca within a clinical setting or within a Western academic model as a remedy to a specific ailment or ailiments is not the same as understanding the way it is used within a ceremonial context, nor within an Indigenous context.

Another category of books and research about ayahuasca focuses on anthropological exploration, ethnographic descriptions of visits to meet ayahuasca healers, and books that explore the esoteric aspects of ayahuasca. Many of these books discussing ayahuasca seem to be based on speculative assumptions about the origins of ayahuasca and the implications of using plant medicines. These authors do not necessarily dig into the potential social impact ayahuasca could have, nor on the ancient traditions from which ayahuasca comes. While many of these books are interesting and document cultures far from my own, I find that too many people read them and create a romanticized version of Indigenous peoples in South America and avoid looking at the context in which Indigenous peoples live, and social, environmental, and political challenges these peoples face. Furthermore, when people focus only on overly romantic versions of ayahuasca cultures, they avoid doing their own critical reflection work on themselves, which I argue is one of the main purposes of ayahuasca ceremonies.

Several beautiful books have been published that contain the art and commentaries of Pablo Amaringo, a celebrated ayahuasca artist from Pucallpa, Peru (Eduardo, Luna, & Amaringo, 1999; Charing, Cloudsley, & Amaringo, 2011). These books are powerful documentaries of the master artist and ayahuasca healer, Amaringo. Throughout the world Amaringo's paintings are associated with ayahuasca and the stunning images he has created document his visions in ayahuasca ceremonies. Amaringo (in Charing, Cloudsley, & Amaringo, 2011) articulates his spirit vision for life, inspired by ayahuasca: "The best thing you can leave is a seed for others to work with. I'm not just a person: I'm a spiritual person. I always communicate with the great universal force, which is the rock of perfection—Dios— that I have seen in my ayahuasca visions, and which has always spoken to me" (p. 1). Amaringo's stories, however, are not about social issues. Instead, they are all directly related to ayahuasca ceremonies and his visions during his experiences as a healer and ceremony leader.

My goal in including a brief analysis of a few styles and types of literature commonly available about ayahuasca is not to point the finger or to criticize ayahuasca writers and researchers, but to show the gap in the literature that I feel is missing from the public conversation about ayahuasca; that being the social change potential ayahuasca ceremonies may provide. One camp of people put forth the idea that healing must only take place on an individual basis, and that by healing one person, those who are healed go on to heal the greater society and world. This notion of individual healing is something I fully support. However, after talking to hundreds, if not thousands, of people who work with plant medicines, I can definitively say that the social change aspects of plant medicines and awareness of the destruction caused by Western hegemony tend to be missing from the general conversation and topics of interest discussed by ceremony participants in several ayahuasca communities within the United States. The discussions about Western hegemony and the potential for social change also seems to be missing in popular discussion groups online, where some groups seem more interested in learning how to make ayahuasca analogs at home, and how to synthesize DMT (Di-Methyl Tryptamine) than working seriously and in a disciplined ceremonial manner, and then facing their attention outwards to the greater world and challenging many of the social ills of our time caused by Western hegemony.

WHAT IS AYAGOGY?

I made up the term ayagogy to represent my work because it frames ayahuasca and ayahuasca ceremonies as a learning and educational model. As an educator, I propose that ayahuasca ceremonies are themselves a format for adult learning, and the catalyst for this learning and teaching is the plant teacher ayahuasca. Ayagogy integrates adult learning, the development of critical consciousness, Indigenous models for learning, and elements of transformational learning into its own unique method of healing and learning.

Many people associate the term pedagogy with the practice teaching. The term pedagogy, however, implies teaching children, and teaching in a hierarchical fashion within a classroom context. According to Armour-Thomas and Gordon (2012), "pedagogy constitutes a broad range of elements in curriculum, assessment and instruction that teachers orchestrate and use to promote student learning" (p. 1). Pedagogy in the case of teaching children within a classroom context implies teaching to a preset curriculum, within an institutional context that is generally prescribed, including what and how the materials are taught (Alexander, 2004, p. 11). Brazilian educator Paulo Freire (2004) describes the Western model of teaching as the banking concept of education, whereby students are viewed as passive recepticles who are "filled" with knowledge. A few of the assumptions of this style of education are that, "The teacher teaches and the students are taught; the teacher knows everything and the students know nothing; the teacher talks and the students listen-meekly" (p. 73).

These examples from Freire and others depict some of the problems associating ayahuasca learning with pedagogy. In contrast, ayahuasca instructs adults to deeply understanding themselves and the world around them. Ayahuasca ceremonies as an educational model is able to help adults learn profound lessons about themselves, and then apply these lessons to living a more purposeful life.

In contrast to pedagogy, Knowles (1980) argues that adult education should be focused on self-actualization, and the learning process should include the emotional, intellectual, and psychological components of a person. Knowles created the term andragogy, to focus on a distinct educational model for adults. Andragogy includes four distinct principles that separate it from pedagogy (Knowles, 1970):

    1. Movement from dependence to self-direction.

    2. Movement from passive learning to experiential, simulation, and problem-solving learning.

    3. Movement from prescriptive learning from outside (such as prescribed by school curriculums), towards learning that is applicable and important to the individual.

    4. Adult learning is a process to develop competency to achive full potential. (pp 43-44).

Andragogy, however, does not necessarily include a critical component. In other words, andragogy is a model for adult learning that is adult-centered and experiential in nature, though not necessarily including the development of critical thinking skills, or unmasking institutional forms of power that drive, and in the process erode, self-determination and individual freedom. One of the central ideas found within the work of Paulo Freire is the concept of "conscientization," or the process of developing critical awareness of one's self (Freire, 2004). "Critical" in this context means critical of oppressive institutional forces, including classism, racism, social, political, and capitalistic influences (Mezirow, 1981).

Freire also suggests that an essential part of liberation is to seek out, through rigorous self-examination, forms of oppression that have been have unconsciously adopted. These forms of oppression are akin to various forms of covert hegemonic forces that dictate belief at such a prominent cultural level that individuals do not even realize their own thoughts and beliefs are complicit with hegemonic forces. The process of liberation, according to Freire, starts with developing criticality to foster self-determination. Self-determination in this case does not refer to independence of a country or a Nation-state, but individuals finding authentic freedom from oppressive forces.

Indigenous models of experiential and emotional learning. When people experience ayahuasca, it is not on a conceptual or theoretical level; it is a unique direct experience. Deloria and Wildcat (2001) assert that sacredness among Indigenous peoples is felt through direct experience, and through direct actions. The Indigenous worldview, and the significance it gives to experiential learning, contrasts with Western academic models of learning. Furthermore, an important aspect of Indigenous experiential learning is learning how to work with emotions, specifically fear. Jacobs (1998) explains that traditional cultures intentionally use fear within a learning context to help people expand and learn how to utilize emotions in the learning process. Indigenous people understand fear and learn how to work with it as a way to become liberated from its limitations (p. 156). The ayahuasca experience provides emotional learning, teaching, and healing through direct experience. Academic models of learning tend to ignore the role of emotion in the learning process and ignore the visceral-level reaction individuals feel in relation to various forms of oppression and injustice. The ayahuasca ceremony leader I interviewed for this book summed up the ayahuasca process in the following way: "The medicine works as a galvanizing experience. It pulverizes the ego and challenges people to look more deeply at their ideas and illusions of what life is like. It is a disorienting experience for many people, but the challenges always lead to more freedom." The ayahuasca experience in this case provides movement away from the trappings of Western hegemony towards liberation.

Transformational learning. The field of transformational learning also aims to help individuals transform the way they view the world, themselves, and their outer actions. Mezirow (1996) describes this transformational process as, "A perspective transformation leads to a more fully developed (more functional) frame of reference . . . one that is more (a) inclusive, (b) differentiating, (c) permeable, (d) critically reflective, and (e) integrative of experience" (p. 163). O'Sullivan (2003) suggests, "Transformative learning involves experiencing a deep, structural shift in the basic premises of thought, feelings, and actions. It is a shift of consciousness that dramatically and irreversibly alters our way of being in the world (p. 203). Both transformational learning as well as the ayahuasca experience point to similar forms of transformation, generated from different stimuli.

Ayagogy: A call to action

As Freire (2004) argues, individuals must become aware of their own oppression and the mechanisms of oppression before they can challenge it. As a result, it is crtical that discussions about oppressive forces be included in discussions of the impact and change potential associated with plant medicines. Part of the process of awareness of oppressive structures is to apply language and dialogue to understanding these mechanisms. This book is an attempt to open up those discussions and explore different ways of looking at how ayahuasca ceremonies may work as a social change agent and educational model. As the poet Adrienne Rich (1979) suggests, "In a world where language and naming are power, silence is oppression, is violence" (p. 184). As inspired by Rich, the goals of this book are to name the oppressive structures created by hegemony, in particular Western hegemony, and to hopefully start a series of dialogs that may result in movements away from Western hegemony. In this case, the other goal is to discuss ayahuasca as a potential social change agent and learning model.

Overview of the book

In Chapter 1, I begin to explore the problem, as I see it. Specifically, that the world is in turmoil, with a collision of forces hitting at once: from environmental destruction to extinction of animals and plants. Many of the problems facing us today stem from Westernization, specifically Western hegemony (which will be defined and explored in depth in the next chapter). One solution to Westernization and Western hegemony may be found within Indigenous wisdom and Indigenous technologies, specifically ayahuasca. Ayahuasca is explored and defined and ayahuasca healing techniques described, along with issues related to ayahuasca and legality. My own personal interest in ayahuasca as a social change agent, along with my background, is included.

The purpose of Chapter 2 is to explore, define, and examine in-depth the meanings of hegemony, Western hegemony, and colonization. These distinctions are critical to my book, and to my work, so many concrete examples are included, and my explanations draw from many sources to illustrate how these forms of domination work and operate. I have struggled quite a bit to understand how hegemony functions. As a result, I wanted to offer illustrations in plain language, hopefully avoiding as much academic jargon as possible, so that you can also understand and clearly see how these forces affect your life and may influence your own thinking and worldview.

In Chapter 3, I present the data from my ayahuasca research project. My research included several steps, and each one included gathering data about ayahuasca and people's experiences with ayahuasca. Data is included from the short-qualitative interviews with people who have worked with ayahuasca, as well as data from the in-depth qualitative interviews with an ayahuasca ceremony leader, and comments left from people who completed a scaled quantitative questionnaire. The data from the qualitative data is presented thematically, and serves to demonstrate my coding process.

In Chapter 4, I present the major findings of my research study, and the focus of this book. I explore and present the 5 antidotal movements away from Western hegemony, including: Antidote 1: Movement from the personal trappings of Western hegemony towards self-determination.

Antidote 2: Movement from individuality and "survival of the fittest" toward relationality and kinship-focused.

Antidote 3: Movement from anthropocentrism towards an anthropomorphic view of the natural world.

Antidote 4: Movement from being materially and commodity focused towards meaning and purpose found outside of consumerism and commodification.

Antidote 5: Movement from unconsciousness regarding political and social influences, towards criticality, or even rejection of these influences. This chapter also includes a powerful interview with Sonbonfu Some. I have also included a significant interview with Michael Yellowbird, a widely published author and professor of Indigenous studies at North Dakota State University. This chapter concludes with an exploration of the Western worldview versus an Indigenous worldview.

Chapter 5 features my most recent research interviews with experts in the field of ayahuasca, psychedelic, and entheogen studies. I have included my interviews with Rick Strassman, one of the foremost authorities on psychedelic studies and author of a groundbreaking study on DMT, Alan Shoemaker, host of the annual International Amazonian Shamanism Conference in Peru, and founder of the Soga Del Alma Church (Vine of the Soul). I am also including my interview with Rak Razam an 'experiential' journalist, writing about and helping shape the emergence of a new cultural paradigm in the 21st century, author of the book Aya awakenings: A shamanic odyssey.

In Chapter 6, I look at some of the problems ayahuasca, specifically how ayahuasca is far from a perfect solution to Westernization. Ayahuasca, and ayahuasca culture worldwide presents its own set of challenges, people who exploit others, corrupt organizations, attracts its own share of unethical people, and certainly not beyond critique. In this chapter, I look at issues such as cultural appropriation, romanticization of Indigenous peoples (especially those in South America connected to ayahuasca cultures), the influence of Christianity on the legality of ayahuasca worldwide and its influence on how ayahuasca ceremonies are conducted, the commodification of ayahuasca ceremonies, including ayahuasca tourism, abuse of power by ayahuasca leaders, including the exploitation of women, psychonauts, and lastly, how many people lack post-ceremony social support, and therefore struggle to integrate healing and lessons from the ayahuasca work.

CHAPTER 1: Overview

I now do it. I make it.
With this song, I connect with the ayahuasca.
With much love in my body, mind, spirit, and with the body, mind,
and spirit of everyone in the group.
I connect with the medicine of ayahuasca to each of you.
I open the great vision of the medicine,
and give strength to our bodies, and minds.
With this medicine I open the world of peace and happiness for all.
(Shipibo ayahuasca ceremony song translated to English, in Gile, 2008)

CONTEXTUALIZING THE PROBLEM

As a citizen of Mother Earth, I try to walk my life path with open eyes and a soft heart, but sometimes the oppression, inequities, exploitation, ecological destruction, and violence overwhelm my senses. When this happens, I find solace in the wisdom of Indigenous Peoples who have long warned of the tragic consequences relating to the growing imbalances in the world. For example, the Hopi term, koyaanisqatsi translates as "life in turmoil," "life disintegrating," and "crazy life" (David, 2003, p. 1). Their giving voice and recognition to the problem makes me realize I am not alone in my concerns. In 1977, A Basic Call to Consciousness (in Sheehy, 1999) was written by members of the Iroquois tribe and presented at the 1977 United Nations Conference on Indigenous Peoples. The document states, "The technologies and social systems which destroyed the animal and the plant life are destroying the Native people" (p. 78). Deloria (1973) concludes, "The imminent and expected destruction of the life cycle of world ecology can be prevented by a radical shift in outlook...Making this shift in viewpoint is essentially religious, not economic or political" (p. 290). Deloria's statement drives home the significance of Indigenous viewpoints and the urgency to protect the natural world.

Similar assertions are being made by more and more Western scholars who suggest Indigenous wisdom may be a possible solution to the confluences of forces, at this moment in history, seen as the solution. For example, MIT professor Noam Chomsky writes,

> the grim prognosis for life on this planet is the consequence of a few centuries of forgetting what traditional societies knew, and the surviving ones still recognize. We must nurture and preserve our common possession, the traditional commons, for future generations, and this must be one of our highest values, or we are all doomed. To regain this sensibility from those who have preserved it we must pay careful attention to their understanding and practices. (in Jacobs, 2013, p. back cover)

The irony related to the growing number of Western people who are coming to recognize the importance of Indigenous wisdom is that, on the one hand, Indigenous wisdom is becoming more obscure and disappearing as Indigenous elders pass away, oftentimes without a new generation wanting to understand these ancient teachings and pursue Indigenous wisdom. At the same time, forces of Western hegemony and neoliberalism are creating more oppression, causing an ever-widening gap between those who have access to wealth and resources, and those who do not. The result is a variety of social, economic, political, and environmental conflicts at a time in which there seems to be little opportunity for Indigenous wisdom to play out.

This book examines one possible option for implementing Indigenous wisdom as a solution to Western cultural hegemony in its various forms. It explores the possibility that ancient wisdom found in the hallucinogenic brew ayahuasca, found in the upper Amazon of South America, may be a potential antidote to Western hegemony. The ayahuasca experience, I hypothesize, may have more potential for creating social awareness and providing motivation for life-changing behaviors than educational social change movements, such as critical pedagogy. The ayahuasca experience also seems to have the potential to work more effectively than Western psychotherapy, in terms of helping people heal from trauma, depression, anxiety, and internal battles. I am referring to the ayahuasca experience as the ceremonial use of ayahuasca. Later in this chapter, I define ayahuasca and go into greater detail about its ceremonial uses. This book looks at how and if ceremonies with the "plant medicine teacher" known as ayahuasca works to help people to become more aware of the subtle power of Western hegemony and take actions to move away from these destructive forces. This is not to suggest that ayahuasca is some panacea, especially in the West. In Chapter 6, I investigate ways that the ayahuasca experience for Western participants may be a continuation or an expression of hegemony, as well as a counter to it.

Ayahuasca in Popular Culture

Over the past decade, there has been a sharp increase in interest in ayahuasca noted in the West, specifically in the United States. A quick Google search shows dozens of centers in South America advertising ayahuasca retreats to people from the West, offering plush retreats with English-speaking ayahuasca healers. Twenty years ago, ayahuasca was relatively unknown and rarely mentioned within popular culture. The National Geographic television network has documented several ayahuasca ceremonies on their television shows, such as their Drugs Inc. series. In 2014, the New York Times ran an article describing one person's account of attending an ayahuasca ceremony (Morris, 2014). Anthony Bourdain (2013) filmed his experiences taking ayahuasca as part of his travel show, Parts Unknown. During season 4 of the television show Weeds, the star drinks ayahuasca with her boyfriend. Jennifer Aniston drinks ayahuasca in the romantic comedy called Wanderlust. These examples of ayahuasca coverage within popular culture point to some of the more dramatic elements of the ayahuasca such as vomiting, unusual visions and hallucinations, and the therapeutic and existential value of the ceremonies. There is no discussion of the possible social or political changes that could arise from ayahuasca usage, which is what my book explores.

NBC News correspondent Brian Alexander (2014) stated that Lindsay Lohan has used ayahuasca to cope with depression. Godfrey (2014) discussed the healing process for post-traumatic stress disorder CNN anchor Amber Lyon experienced using ayahuasca and is now a proponent. According to Bain (2013), celebrities such as Paul Simon and Tori Amos have used ayahuasca and publically spoken about the benefits of the experience. In an interview in Rolling Stone magazine 20 years ago, Sting said, "it's not a frivolous pursuit...there's a certain amount of dread attached to taking it — you have a hallucinogenic trip that deals with death and your mortality. So it's quite an ordeal" (Dunn, 1998, p. 26). Ayahuasca has been discussed in pop culture women's magazines Elle (Cohen, 2014) and Marie Claire (Aguirre, 2014). Men's Journal has written about ayahuasca as well (Zaitchik, 2013).

One problem with discussions about ayahuasca in popular media is that various forms of Western media tend to support Western hegemonic forces. Western media tends to exist to sell products and frame experience in terms of their commodity value. Media coverage of ayahuasca ultimately comes down to creating television shows for people to watch and magazines for people to purchase and read, and has very little to do with connecting to the spirit of ayahuasca. Furthermore, looking to famous people to learn about ayahuasca supports another hegemonic structure which entails social dichotomy whereby those with status can dictate to those without status how to live their lives, which products to buy, which experiences to explore, and so on. The assumption is that if an Indigenous person recommends people experience ayahuasca, s/he is not credible, but somehow a Hollywood celebrity is credible, simply because s/he is famous.

PERSONAL STATEMENT

My parents were both civil rights activists. As a kid, topics such as the Civil Rights Movement, the Women's Movement, sexism, racism, and classism were regularly discussed over the dinner table and became part of my awareness. As a teenager, being part of the American punk rock movement of the 1980s highlighted a mountain of discontent, hopelessness, and frustration felt by myself and my peers towards oppressive governmental policies and forces that promote war, poverty, and the dumbing down of America. Seeing bands such as Millions of Dead Cops (MDC), Black Flag, the Dicks, along with fanzine culture, opened my mind up to protest movements, and the questioning of authority and institutional hierarchies. The punk rock movement showed me that anyone could play music, and that authentic self-expression, outside of the mainstream, be it through music, visual art, poetry, or any other form, could be deeply meaningful. On a larger contextual level, seeing bands almost every weekend and playing in a punk band with my friends expanded my mind even more about the idea that happiness could exist outside of materialism, simply through the act of creativity. It also opened my mind to see that pursing one's passion could exist outside of materialism and commodification. I attended a high school named after Malcolm X, called Malcolm Shabazz-High that offered courses about civil rights, American Indian history, and social activism. Social activism and social change were themes and values that some people participating in the American punk rock movement aspired to, and may have been the impetus for some forward progress and incremental political and social changes. Unfortunately, these Western models of protest and social change have proven to be relatively ineffective at fighting Western hegemony. While many musicians in famous punk bands may have been able to maintain a living outside the status quo, and inspired others to live and work in non-traditonal occupations and lifestyles, Western hegemony may be more destructive than it was in the 1980s. Furthermore, these social change models were conceived within a Western framework and worldview, along with Western models of politics and justice, and are steeped in Western beliefs and values. As a result, they have not transformed the deeper structure of oppression connected to the power of hegemony. In fact, the state of the planet continues to worsen. Missing from these change models is the power of Indigenous wisdom to challenge the Western worldview. An example of implementing change models from Indigenous peoples is the 2011 "Mother Earth Law" enacted in Bolivia, which grants rights to the earth as equal to humans. Indigenous wisdom and the Indigenous worldview hold important keys to creating sustainable and lasting social changes and to challenging Western hegemony.

I did not set out to study Western hegemony, nor did I ever intend to examine the effects of ayahuasca. In 2005, after my mother died, I went on a trip to Peru, where I experienced ayahuasca. Being in a jungle environment with elders who have been leading ayahuasca ceremonies for decades, in the natural habitat where ayahuasca grows freely and has been brewed and used for thousands of years, was a life-changing experience. While I only visited the area for a short time, the experience was galvanizing to my previous views of the world and my part in it. I walked away with reverence not only for the plant teacher ayahuasca, but reverence for the power and insight of leaders and elders and their knowledge and depth, the beauty and power of the ayahuasca songs, and the cultural traditions surrounding ayahuasca. These experiences with ayahuasca in Peru showed me many ways in which I was previously unconscious of my own lack of relationship to the natural world. These experiences with ayahuasca showed me ways of looking more deeply at oppression on many different levels, and opened my eyes to the potential ayahuasca might have as a cultural change agent.

The research I conducted for my master's degree thesis focused on exploring questions related to transformational learning. Specifically, I was interested in the tension points between personal transformational learning and social transformative acts, including social activism. The tension points include the following: Which one creates the most change? Is transformation most effective as an "outside-in" process (transform a culture and, in the process, we will be transformed)? Or is transformational learning most effective "inside-out" (as we transform and become more awake and aware people, our world will transform in the process)? These tension points seemed at the time to be polar opposites. An individual could focus on transforming himself or herself, on one hand, and therefore primarily have an individualistic worldview. Or, a person could focus outside himself or herself and exclusively look at political and social change. I could not see middle ground at the time, or examples of theories that posited models that showed the intersections between the two. My experiences in Peru with ayahuasca began to open my mind to the grey areas in between these two views. The ayahuasca experience may possibly provide an opening both to provide opportunities to help individuals heal and change from inside out and also move towards becoming social change agents by providing more awareness of hegemonic oppression and opportunities to combat it.

My early doctoral research focused on examining issues related to the cultural preservation of Indigenous peoples. In my view, the Internet and Internet culture seem to be in opposition to Indigenous cultural wisdom, especially Indigenous rituals and ceremonies; specifically, how the process of digitization tends to remove people from direct experience and experiential learning situations. For Indigenous peoples, this seems to imply another form of assimilation. Technology is not neutral, but instead promotes Euro-American values (McLoughlin, 1999, p. 236). The Internet has promoted a form of globalization of local culture. Some have referred to globalization as the "McDonaldization" of symbolic life (Little, Holmes, & Grieco, 2001, p. 354), while Indigenous wisdom traditions are based on having direct and personal experiences as part of the premise of rituals, ceremonies, and various forms of Indigenous educational systems (Cajete, 1994). How can we, given the worldwide use of computer-based technologies, hold onto rituals and ceremonies that center around direct experiences, especially experience-based learning that creates awareness and appreciation for the earth and the natural world? I couldn't find many solutions to this question, only examples of cultural loss and struggle, which left me feeling pessimistic about the potential to remedy the challenges created by Internet culture. I was inspired by the Idle No More protest movement, organized by Indigenous women in Canada. This protest movement was organized on Facebook and spread all over the world, inciting different types of protests, in particular, environmental protests, around the world on behalf of Indigenous causes.

Another theme that inspired me to look at Western hegemony as a destructive force is the prevalence of the stealing of Indigenous artistic, spiritual, and cultural traditions by the West. This type of misappropriation is another threat to Indigenous wisdom that is not commonly discussed. As I looked at American Indians and other Indigenous groups, I found what seemed to be endless examples of Indigenous cultures and peoples being exploited and taken advantage of by Western hegemons, which are powerful entities within the structure of hegemony. In these examples of Indigenous peoples being exploited there always seems to be a profit motive driving the exploitation, this underlying drive for profit without concern of how many people are harmed, the natural world that is destroyed, and the future damage caused by this drive for profit are all examples of hegemony.

In 2012, I conducted a pilot study, attempting to interview Indigenous people on how the Internet and computer-based technologies could possibly be used to preserve their culture/s and cultural wisdom. I had hoped to interview some of the founders of the American Indian Movement (AIM); some of these American Indian elders live near me in Minneapolis, Minnesota. I sent out dozens of requests to American Indians in the United States, including educators, those in academia, spiritual elders, and students. Only two people responded to the request for interviews. The first was a professor at University of Wisconsin-Madison in the American Indian Studies Department, Patty Loew, and the other, controversial activist and scholar Ward Churchill. During the interview, Churchill argued, "The idea that American imperialism might exist and that America is the hub of the empirical matrix at this point in the globalization process, that's all well and good. But there is globalization of other things, this techno-net being a key component of it" (personal communications, November 4, 2012). Churchill's interview all came back to topics related to hegemony. My interview with him was part of my refocusing my work to hegemony and away from technology.

The lack of response to my interview requests left me puzzled about why my interview requests were being ignored. I had been ignorant to the many ways in which Indigenous people have been exploited and taken advantage of by researchers. No wonder no American Indians wanted me to interview them or participate in any more academic research studies by someone who is an outsider to their community. I then began to look at the extensive history of Western researchers and Western research methods mistreating Indigenous peoples and Indigenous communities (Kovach, 2009; Schnarch, 2004; Smith, 1999; Wilson, 2008). Research abuse has taken many forms, including harming human subjects during the research process, profiting from Indigenous knowledge, taking funeral and burial objects, and various forms of biocolonialism.

Awareness of research abuse led me to decolonizing methodologies, in particular the work of Linda Tuhiwai Smith (1999). Her work and the work of others related to decolonizing methodologies brought biases within the Western academic model of scholarship to the forefront of my awareness. Smith, who is associated with Maori people of New Zealand, and other Indigenous scholars who discuss biases within Western academia, show how Western methodologies tend to be biased in their own epistemological views and tend to elevate their own methods and sense of validity above those of other cultures and cultural ways of knowing. In the process of elevating their own views, Western epistemological views tend to devalue Indigenous knowledge and ways of knowing (Kovach, 2009; Smith, 1999).

These Western biases all point to various forms of Western hegemony that I previously could not see. I could see pieces of the puzzle, but the decolonizing methodologies clearly show bias that I did not find in the critical pedagogy nor critical theory texts and theories to which I had previously been exposed. The other influential person in my understanding of hegemony and Western hegemony has been my mentor in my doctoral program, Four Arrows. Through many lengthy discussions, email exchanges (sometimes heated), and his own body of research, I've come to see and believe that the biggest challenges to citizens of the world, the environment, and the ecosystem, are the forces of hegemony which shape the world more than the eye can see. These destructive forces work hard to create a stratified world, which manipulates people and takes away their freedom. I can now clearly see how hegemony, in particular Western hegemony, shapes my life, and how cultural and institutional forces shape my daily life and restrict my freedom.

My gender, class, ethnicity, and geography influence my personal biases in the research process and how this book was conceived. As a Jewish male, growing up in Madison, Wisconsin, from a fairly intact home with a mother who had a master's degree in social work and a father who had a Ph.D. in social work, I grew up with a very different worldview than an Indigenous person. I cannot really understand what elders in the ayahuasca ceremonies experience, or understand. At the same time, I have gone to considerable lengths to be exposed to and to understand Indigenous peoples, some of their rituals, ceremonies, and teachings.

In the process of examining my own biases and my own internal landscape, I came to the conclusion that ayahuasca may be one of the forces that could combat Western hegemony. Even making the slightest dent in weakening Western hegemony was a worthy dissertation research goal and the driving force for me publishing this book. Through my research process, it has become impossible for me to live in denial any longer, and pretend the oppressive forces of Western hegemony do not exist and influence nearly every aspect of daily life. The only conclusion I draw is that a radical approach must be taken. A radical approach to me suggests implementing solutions and wisdom found within an Indigenous context. The Indigenous plant teacher ayahuasca may have the power to shift human consciousness, and encourage individuals to re-examine their relationships, values, and lives. I believe ayahuasca may be a radical approach to combatting Western hegemony. This dissertation explores the question of how the ayahuasca experience may be a potential antidote to Western hegemony, even though ayahuasca and other Indigenous solutions are not normally thought of as solutions to the effects of Western hegemony.

INDIGENOUS KNOWLEDGE

The field of Indigenous research and Indigenous knowledge is wide and deep. Various theorists discuss and refer to various types of Indigenous "knowing," wisdom, healing, and understanding. Indigenous knowledge is holistic, relational, and sacred (Kincheloe & Steinberg, 2008). At the same time, Indigenous knowledge is locally oriented and unique to each culture and society (Dei, Hall, & Rosenberg, 2000). According to Semali (1999a), "Indigenous knowledge does not derive its origins or meaning from the individual but from the collective epistemological understanding and rationalization of the community" (p. 309). Indigenous peoples have produced and constructed various cosmologies, ontologies, and epistemologies that involve knowledge protection about plant and animal life, medicines and remedies, historical information, and cultural knowledge (Mercer, Kelman, Taranis, & Suchet-Pearson, 2009). As a body of knowledge, Indigenous knowledge is distinct from modern, scientific, formal knowledge (Semali 1999b, Kincheloe & Steinberg, 2008). Indigenous knowledge is experiential, oral, personal, holistic, and conveyed through metaphoric language and narrative. Indigenous knowledge and knowing involves making connections between things, valuing relationships, storytelling, and artistic expression (Cajete, 1994; Castellano, 2000; Maurial, 1999). Indigenous knowledge is constantly evolving, updated, and reinvented by Indigenous peoples (Fletcher, 2004). This exploration of Indigenous knowledge is included as a way to more deeply understand the importance and depth of Indigenous knowledge. At the same time, most discussions of Indigenous knowledge do not discuss specific healing rituals such as the ayahuasca ceremonial experience.

About Ayahuasca And Ayahuasca Ceremonies

Ayahuasca

Ayahuasca is a hallucinogenic drink that is consumed throughout the upper Amazon region in South America including Peru, Colombia, Bolivia, and Ecuador, for medicinal and spiritual benefits (Freedland & Mansbach, 1999). Ayahuasca is predominantly used by Indigenous Amazonian tribes and by ayahuasca healers who use ayahuasca to treat a variety of ailments, including physical, spiritual, and emotional illnesses. Since the 1990s, usage has spread to the United States, Europe, and Asia. According to the Ethnobotanical Stewardship Council (2014), each year approximately 100,000 people visit Peru specifically to drink ayahuasca. Anthropological evidence of ayahuasca usage can be dated to 2000 BC (McKenna, D. 2004; Barbosa, Mizumoto, Bogenschutz, & Strassman, 2012). The term ayahuasca (pronounced ah-yuh-wah-sku) is a Quechua word meaning "vine of the dead" (Shanon, 2002), although other definitions of ayahuasca include, "vine of visions" and "vine of the soul" (Mizrach, 2003). It is commonly understood that aya means spirit or ancestor and waska refers to vine (Luna, 2011, p. 3). Ayahuasca is also known under several other names as well including caapi, yage, hosca, and daime (Grob et al., 1996; Rivier & Lindgren, (1972).

For many Indigenous communities in the upper Amazon, ayahuasca influences nearly every aspect of daily life. Schultes (1982), an early researcher in the study of South American psychoactive plants, emphasized the significance of ayahuasca:

> Probably no other New World hallucinogen – even peyote – alters consciousness in ways that have been so deeply and completely evaluated and interpreted. Caapi (ayahuasca) truly enters into every aspect of living. It reaches into prenatal life, influences life after death, operates during earthly existence, plays roles not only in health and sickness, but in relations between individuals, villages and tribes, in peace and war, at home and in travel, in hunting and in agriculture. In fact, one can name hardly any aspect of living or dying, wakefulness or sleep, where caapi hallucinogens do not play a vital, nay, overwhelming, role. (p. 205)

The ayahuasca brew itself is a combination of two essential ingredients, the first being the ayahuasca vine (Banisteriopis caapi), along with the leafy plant chacruna (Psychotria viridis). Chacruna contains the psychoactive dimethyltryptamine (DMT) (D. McKenna, 1998). DMT is similar in structure to the neurotransmitter serotonin and alters brain chemistry along the lines of other natural hallucinogens (Metzner, 2005; Riba et al., 2003). The DMT found in the chacruna would normally be destroyed in the digestive system by a chemical called mono-amine oxidase, rendering the ayahuasca brew ineffective. However, the ayahuasca vine itself (Baniseriopis caapi) contains a mono-amine oxidase inhibitor (MAOI), that allows the DMT to be digested, absorbed, pass the blood-brain barrier, and create an altered state of consciousness (Grob, 2005). According to Winkelman (2005), "Ayahuasca is considered to be the most widely employed hallucinogen in Amazonia, with combinations based on the Banisteriopsis genus found in more than 70 different ethnic groups representing 20 language families in the Amazon basin and other areas of South America" (p. 210). The origins of ayahuasca usage are mysterious. Some researchers assert that ayahuasca has been used for over 5,000 years. Yet, ayahuasca scholar Beyer (2012) argues that ayahuasca usage may have begun as recently as the 17th century.

Using Respectful Terminology to Discuss Ayahuasca. It is important that I be respectful of the Indigenous use of plant medicines in how I frame my research and discussions about ayahuasca in this book. In the West, ayahuasca may be considered a drug, yet to the Indigenous peoples of South America, it is considered a sacred plant teacher, a wise elder, and a powerful healer (Harris & Gurel, 2012). Within ayahuasca cultures in South America ayahuasca is considered a plant teacher and a plant medicine. For members of the Santo Daime Church, ayahuasca is their sacrament (Tupper, 2011). Within a traditional context, ayahuasca is known as a living spirit capable of teaching and healing participants. By plant teacher, I am referring to ayahuasca within a traditional context, as a living spirit capable of teaching and healing people. Some ayahuasca traditions refer to ayahuasca as Grandmother Ayahuasca. Given this, gender is a way of referring to the sacred feminine quality of ayahuasca and the reverence given to both the power and wisdom of this plant teacher. This way of working with ayahuasca points to the spiritual quality of the ayahuasca experience and the ways in which ayahuasca ceremony leaders work on various levels of healing, including physical, mental, spiritual, and emotional.

Within this book I use a few different phrases to describe the ayahuasca experience. The first one is ayahuasca ceremony. I describe what happens in a specific ayahuasca ceremony in the next section, but in short, I am referring to the ceremonial use of ayahuasca by a trained ayahuasca leader, not in a recreational context. Rather than use the phrases "take ayahuasca" or "use ayahuasca," I refer to people working with ayahuasca throughout this book. I am using this terminology because within an Indigenous context ayahuasca is revered and viewed as sacred, and part of a long process of serious dedicated work and sacrifice. People who follow an ayahuasca path are usually committed to working on a long-term basis with ayahuasca as a plan teacher. As a result, the term work with seems to best describe their ayahuasca usage. The other terms I use at various parts in this book is calling ayahuasca medicine or references to medicine ceremonies. Referring to ayahuasca, and in some cases, other plant teachers as medicines, again points to these sacred plants being viewed as having the potential to heal people and communities at various levels. Referring to ayahuasca as medicine draws a clear distinction between ayahuasca being viewed as a drug or as something used recreationally versus a sacred medicine that is revered and worked with in a humble way to help individuals heal at various levels.

Ayahuasca Healing Techniques. Ayahuasca ceremony leaders employ a variety of healing techniques during an ayahuasca ceremony. According to Beyer (2007),

First among such substances is, of course, tobacco, which is ingested by indigenous shamans in every conceivable way, and by mestizo shamans primarily by smoking or by drinking cold infusions of tobacco leaves in water. Blowing tobacco smoke onto the body of a patient, or into the body by blowing the smoke into the top of the head, is part of the foundational triad of mestizo shamanic healing — shacapar, rattling; chupar, sucking; and soplar, blowing.

Other common healing techniques within traditional ayahuasca ceremonies are singing sacred songs (icaros), whistling, using sacred perfume as a way to invoke protection, massaging a participant's head or stomach, and sometimes counseling people during ayahuasca ceremonies. The ayahuasca experience is different for each person. Oftentimes people purge during an ayahuasca ceremony. Purging, or as some groups call it "getting well," is viewed as the person letting go of heavy energy or negativity, and is part of the healing process facilitated by the wisdom of ayahuasca. There are generally four groupings of experiences people have during an ayahuasca ceremony. The first are visions, or hallucinations. Visions often include images of snakes or unusual entities, and can be scary and demonic or pleasant and soothing, depending on the ceremony. The second grouping is experiencing ayahuasca on a mental level and describing the experience as more of a dialogue with a wise spirit or a wise being. The third grouping of experiences people report are primarily physical sensations during ayahuasca ceremonies. Physical sensations can be unpleasant or pleasant. Oftentimes people report pain in their stomach or a feeling of "buzzing" in a particular body part. These feelings are supposedly the ayahuasca opening up energy channels and helping the person heal on a physical level. Last, many people experience ayahuasca as though they are in a dream-like state and they simply are relaxed and in and out of wakeful consciousness. This type of healing is said to affect the subtle body of a person and act to heal all levels of healing; physical, mental, emotional, and spiritual. Ayahuasca is also said to happen and be experienced in "waves" throughout a particular night or ceremony. By waves, I am referring to the power and feelings of ayahuasca coming and going throughout a particular night, sometimes very strong and overwhelming and other times barely perceptible. At the same time, people report going through many different sets of experiences (combinations of visions, physical sensations, a dream-like quality, and a dialogue with a more intelligent life form) throughout a particular night.

Ayahuasca is currently used in a variety of ways, including personal growth (Harris & Gurel, 2012; Kjellgren, Eriksson, & Norlander, 2009), healing from trauma (Mate, 2013; Nielson & Megler, 2014), treatment of addictions (Brierley & Davidson, 2012; Mabit, 2007; Thomas, Lucas, Capler, Tupper, & Martin, 2013), and treatment of depression (Palladino, 2009; Sobiecki, 2013).

What Happens During an Ayahuasca Ceremony. Ayahuasca ceremonies are usually led by a leader who conducts the ceremony, employs some or all of the healing techniques listed above, and functions as a facilitator ensuring safety and protection of all of the participants. Ayahuasca ceremonies typically are done in the dark and at night, oftentimes from approximately 10 p.m. until 3:00 a.m. Some traditions start at an earlier time and others start even later and end later. Some ayahuasca ceremonies are done one-on-one with a leader and participant, and others have 25 or more participants. Some traditions start at sunset and go until sunrise the next day. Each tradition is different and each group functions differently. People who experience ayahuasca are generally encouraged to be comfortable during the experience and either lie down and relax or sit up and be quiet and receive the teachings and healings from the ayahuasca. In some traditional ayahuasca traditions, only the ayahuasca shaman would consume the ayahuasca, not the participant. The ayahuasca shaman would consume ayahuasca as part of the process to diagnose and cure illness (Proctor, 2001, p. 15)

There is very little standardization in the format and setting of ayahuasca ceremonies. Some styles of ayahuasca ceremonies are rooted in South American ayahuasca traditions and other ceremonies are more Western-inspired. Some groups in the United States, for instance, play pre-recorded music on an iPod and all of the participants lie down and have their own ayahuasca experience. Some groups, inspired by the Church of Santo Daime, require that participants wear all-white clothes, the men and women are separated, song books are distributed, the lights are kept on, and music is played and everyone is encouraged to sing Christian-inspired songs. The Santo Daime Church, founded in Brazil, is a Christian-based religious organization that consumes ayahuasca as their sacrament. Other groups conduct ayahuasca ceremonies more like they do in rural Peru, where the ayahuasca healer sings icaros and the ceremony is conducted primarily in the dark. There are other groups in places such as Brazil and Colombia who come from their own Indigenous traditions and conduct their ceremonies within their own traditional context, with minimal influence of the West and Western ways of working with ayahuasca. There is a huge variety of settings in which ayahuasca is consumed in Western countries, as well. For a detailed account of the various types of ayahuasca groups and religions I recommend the book, Ayahuaca Religions: A comprehensive bibloiography and critical essays (Labate, De Rose, & dos Santos, 2008). Some yoga centers sponsor ayahuasca sessions, as do some intentional communities. Some people participate in American Indian rituals and ceremonies and also attend ayahuasca ceremonies. There is simply no standard; there are many different templates for ayahuasca ceremonies, some more traditional than others. Some are more rooted in Indigenous structure and some more inspired by Western models of ayahuasca ceremonies. There is also no standardization in terms of strength of ayahuasca; by strength, I am referring to the quantity of DMT that can be found in the actual ayahuasca brew. Some ceremony groups offer large quantities of potent ayahuasca and others offer small quantities of relatively weak ayahuasca; each group is different.

Ayahuasca and Legality. Ayahuasca is legal in Peru, Colombia, Ecuador, and Bolivia. In Brazil, the Federal Government ruled that ayahuasca was legal for religious uses (Barbosa, Mizumoto, Bogenschutz, & Strassman, 2012). Religious use of ayahuasca has also been granted in Canada to the Church of Santo Daime (Tupper, 2009a). In the United States, the Controlled Substance Act (CSA, 2000) bans DMT, mescaline, peyote, heroin, marijuana, and psilocybin (the psychedelic compound found in some mushrooms). DMT is considered a Schedule I drug. In 2006, however, after having a shipment of ayahuasca seized by the government, the Church of Uniao do Vegetal (UDV) in New Mexico first won their case for religious freedom in the Federal District Court of New Mexico, and then in the U.S. Supreme Court in February 2006 (Bullis, 2008). The same religious freedom act allows for American Indians to use peyote legally in their ceremonies in the United States. In 2009, the Santo Daime Church in Ashland, Oregon won a district court case that allows them to legally import ayahuasca and use it in their religious rituals (Labate, MacRae, & Goulart, 2010). However, many people in the United States and in Western countries drink ayahuasca in rituals and ceremonies that are not protected by the religious freedom afforded to Christian-based organizations who can legally use ayahuasca, such as the Church of Santo Daime and Uniao de Vegetal. Allowing only Christian-based organizations to legally work with ayahuasca is an example of hegemony, whereby only dominant and powerful groups can dictate legislation, such as Christian based groups, while non-dominant groups such as Indigenous peoples, are not afforded the same rights.

My goal in the presentation of my research is to avoid framing Westerners who work with ayahuasca as drug users. Throughout my research discussions and presentations, my goal was to be respectful of the participants, and to not diminish their experiences, nor frame their experiences any differently than how they discuss them. In this process, my goal was to make sure I did not apply a Western cultural bias to the ayahuasca experience.

Limitations and Challenges in the Research

Given that there are so many different styles and types of ayahuasca experiences, different styles or methods could certainly produce different experiences for participants. Neither the qualitative interviews nor the quantitative scaled survey addressed the differences in ceremony styles. I do not know if some people who attended a ceremony did so with a trained ayahuasca leader or if they bought the supplies though a website and cooked their own ayahuasca. I do not know if they participated in ceremonies in the jungles of Peru or if they participated in a Santo Daime-inspired ayahuasca ceremony in Chicago. These various types of ceremonies could greatly alter the experiences of the individual and therefore alter how they would respond to the interview questions, and therefore affect the results of the study.

Another limitation is the topic I am researching. Western hegemony itself is difficult to understand and see. As a result it can imply subtle changes, intangible changes, and be so entrenched in personal, spiritual, and cultural understandings that it is challenging to quantify or come up with conclusive evidence to suggest anything about it. At the same time, Indigenous cosmologies and the Indigenous worldview do not necessarily address hegemonic themes overtly; certainly, the ayahuasca literature does not.

An additional limitation is the lack of baseline comparisons to other antidotes to Western hegemony. I am unclear how other plant medicines such as peyote, the San Pedro cactus, mushrooms, or other plant medicines may create more or less antidotal movement away from forms of Western hegemony than ayahuasca. I am also limited in my own biases. I am an outsider researching both the ayahuasca experience and the Indigenous worldview. As a Western person, I have a limited understanding of the Indigenous worldview and of the Indigenous understanding of ayahuasca. These are all limitations to this study and examples of challenges found in the research process.

CHAPTER 2: Hegemoney, Western Hegemony, and Colonization Defined

"In order to understand our own position better and to ultimately act to improve it, we must first immerse ourselves in and understand the very systems of thought, ideas and knowledge that have been instrumental in producing our position."
(Nakata, 1998, p. 4)

    One of the central purposes of this book is to find ways to combat hegemony, in particular Western hegemony. While hegemony affects nearly every aspect of our lives (our careers, our health, our food choices, what we watch on TV, our mental and emotional states, how we relate to others, etc.), its illusive nature makes it difficult to pinpoint, isolate and understand. As a result, hegemony by design is confusing and requires the development of criticality to spot, name, and confront. The purpose of this chapter is to offer definitions, explanations, and many examples of hegemony and Western hegemony, in plain terms, so that you can understand hegemony and how it may affect your life in various ways. I also look at, and explore, the distinctions between colonization, hegemony, and Western hegemony.

Hegemony Defined

    Unlike other terms and distinctions that explain oppression, one succinct definition does not fully express what hegemony means, how it operates, and how it affects individuals on various levels. One of the focal points of hegemony is the process of power transfer and control. Antonio Gramsci coined the term "hegemony" and was able to put words to this concept. Hegemony in the Gramsci sense refers to the bridge between the

Marxist notion of ideology and colonization through commodification—in particular how it affects all aspects of life (Gramsci, 1971; Brookfield, 1995). Gramsci (1971) argues, "Every relationship of `hegemony'...occurs not only within a nation, between the various forces of which the nation is composed, but in the international and world-wide field, between complexes of national and continental civilisations" (p. 182). According to Brookfield (2005), "Hegemony is the process by which we learn to embrace enthusiastically a system of beliefs and practices that end up harming us and working to support the interests of those who have power over us" (p. 93). Katz (2006) suggests, "Hegemony refers to a certain way of life and thought being dominant, which is diffused throughout society to inform norms, values and tastes, political practices, and social relations (p. 335). Four Arrows (2006) explains, "The term [hegemony] thus signifies the ability of the dominant social leaders to cultivate, through largely non-coercive means, a popular worldview that naturalizes their positions in a way that manipulates subordinate classes of people to consent to their own subordination and oppression, thinking that it ultimately serves their best interests" (p. 27). Hegemony also relates to "the process by which ruling elites secure consent to the established political order through the production and diffusion of meanings and values" (Carragee & Roefs, 2004, pp. 221-222). Therefore, from this point of view, hegemony results from a combination of coercion and consent. Consent in this case is generally achieved through cooptation of groups in civil society, resulting in "coercive orthodoxy" (Persaud, 2001, p. 65).

Puchala (2005) explains, "Hegemony connotes the domination of the weak by the strong, the many by the few. It implies the institutionalization of privilege, consequent inequality in the distributions of various values, and the injustices inherent in inequality" (p. 571). According to West (1982), hegemonic culture is "a culture successful at persuading people to consent to their oppression and exploitation" (p. 119). Hegemony occurs in such a complicated manner, and is so immersed in a culture, that it becomes difficult to define and challenge. Hegemonic views of the world simply become the norm until they are so accepted that people stop even questioning that point of view. Therefore, hegemony works on both subtle and gross levels in its all-pervasive nature, referring to a wide variety of patterns and methods in which the ruling group establishes and maintains rule (Robinson, 2005, p. 561). As Newman (1994) proposes, "It becomes nearly impossible to fight when the enemy is embedded in the thoughts and actions one takes and the way they live their lives" (p. 102). All of these definitions give a flavor of what hegemony means and how it may operate on gross and subtle levels.

This examination of hegemony would be remiss to not also include a reference to the work of Foucault in exploring power relations. In particular, institutional forms of power and how they affect individuals, groups, and cultures. Foucault (1980) asserts, "Power reaches into the very grain of individuals, touches their bodies and inserts itself into their actions and attitudes, their discourses, learning processes and everyday lives" (p. 39). This definition of power ties directly into how individuals experience hegemony as an external limitation of individual freedom and constrains on self-determination.

Hegemony and race. Many discussions of oppression, such as racism or sexism, issues tend to be discussed in isolation or simplified to the point where the roots are not traced and the complexity explored and acknowledged. Memmi (2000) poignantly writes, "There is a strange kind of enigma associated with the problem of racism. No one, or almost no one, wishes to see themselves as racist; still, racism persists, real and tenacious" (p. 3). When video showing the African American taxi driver Rodney King being beaten by white police offers in Los Angeles in 1991, riots followed. More recently, when the African American teenager Trayvon Martin was shot in his Florida neighborhood by a white man who said he felt threatened by the child, there was outrage about the murder. In both of these incidents, race was the obvious trigger for protest, outrage, disgust, and signs of an America tearing apart, at war within itself. These were both examples of gross overt and covert forms of racism persisting and demonstrating that even though many forms of racism are not always in the public eye, they remain and persist. Racism persists on institutional, social, educational, and many other levels. The structures that hold racism in place, the "strange enigma" Memmi references, are forms of hegemony, which not only act as racist mechanisms, but drive other forms of oppression in tandem.

Western racial hegemony in the form of racism depicts African Americans, in particular African American men, as dangerous and criminal. This negative depiction occurs in various forms of media, such as a disproportionate number of criminals and "bad" people in TV shows and movies. Legally, there is significant police harassment of African Americans, and a disproportionately high number of minorities imprisoned compared to non-minorities. There are fewer educational opportunities for minorities, and less access to health care. There are multiple social forces, mostly created through hegemony, which hold racism in place in America. Omi & Winant (1994) conclude, "In the U.S., race is present in every institution, every relationship, every individual. This is the case not only for the way society is organized — spatially, culturally, in terms of stratification, etc. — but also for our perceptions and understandings of personal experience" (p. 158).

Another illuminating lens to explore hegemony comes from Peggy McIntosh's seminal work on understanding racism, entitled "White privilege: Unpacking the invisible knapsack," (1989). In her essay, McIntosh describes racism in terms of privileges that go unquestioned—for whites versus non-whites, specifically African Americans and people of color. McIntosh argues, "...Since some hierarchies in our society are interlocking, there was most likely a phenomenon of white privilege which was similarly denied and protected" (p. 1).

These hierarchies McIntosh mentioned are forms of hegemony. McIntosh further explains, "I was taught to see racism only in individual acts of meanness, not in invisible systems conferring dominance of my group" (p. 1). Her essay then offers examples of white privilege such as, "I can go shopping alone most of the time, pretty well assured that I will not be followed or harassed. I can turn on the television or open the front page of the paper and see people of my race widely represented. I can be sure that my children will be given curricular materials that testify to the existence of their race" (p. 2). These are just a few of the forty-six examples. McIntosh's work fits in with a discussion about hegemony because it points to institutions and social forces that exert power and oppresses others, yet cannot be superficially seen or noticed. The combined forces of racial oppression are not obvious and take a deeper look to notice, just like hegemony. Her writing is so powerful because it highlights a set of issues which otherwise would be difficult to illustrate. By noticing the privileges whites have, it shows how through hegemony, American culture is often designed in a racist manner.

Hegemony, stratification, and sexism. Taking cues from McIntosh to explore hegemony can be useful in noticing a form of oppression that becomes so entrenched in cultural values and supported by cultural beliefs that it becomes challenging to notice. While McIntosh focuses her essay on white privilege and points to some of the ways racism plays out in terms of benefits for whites and therefore puts those from other cultures at a deficit, the lens could just as easily explore how sexism, homophobia, and classism all function in a similar manner. The same sets of corresponding cultural institutions create situations that promote forms of stratification.

For instance, sexism, particularly the myriad of ways in which women are treated poorly and discounted, has been widely documented. Yet cultural hegemony has kept various forms of sexism in place, such as in the demeaning media depictions of women, lower pay for women in the jobs marketplace, and religious misogyny. Furthermore, rape, rape culture and over-sexualization of women, in particular, young women and girls. In addition, notions of beauty reducing women to sex objects as opposed to being valued for their intellect or other forms of capability. These examples of sexism, and many others, are unfortunately commonplace (Peters & Wolper, 1995; UNO, 2010). As LaDuke (1999), an Indigenous activist, concludes:

> We, collectively, find that we (women) are often in the role of the prey, to a predator society, whether for sexual discrimination, exploitation, sterilization, absence of control over our bodies, or being the subjects of repressive laws and legislation in which we have no voice. This occurs on an individual level, but equally and more significantly on a societal level (p. 42).

All of these examples mentioned by LaDuke offer ways of looking at hegemony and how it operates. These all show the complexity of hegemony and how it functions. LaDuke's comments suggest that sexism happens on multiple institutional levels simultaneously. Sexism and mistreatment of women is particularly severe for Indigenous women.

WESTERN HEGEMONY

While I discussed hegemony earlier in more general terms, Western hegemony is a specific form of hegemony referring to Western values and culture operating as forms of domination and colonization on a worldwide level. At the heart of Western hegemony is Eurocentrism. Eurocentrism, in this case, implies the spread of European values, political systems, culture, language, Judeo-Christian beliefs, laws, philosophy, and epistemologies (NWAC, 2003, pp. 7-8)

There are multiple components that make up Western hegemony. Western knowledge and Western models of knowledge tend to position itself as the authority in areas such as learning and education. In the process, a polarized view of the world is accepted whereby Western, or in this case Eurocentric models of knowledge, are put forth as the only "valid" models. The result is that non-European ways of knowing are often trivialized and seen as simplistic and backward (Kovach, 2010, Wilson, 2008). As Blaut (1993) explains, "Eurocentric thought asserts that only Europeans can progress and that Indigenous peoples are frozen in time, guided by knowledge systems that reinforce the past and do not look towards the future" (p. 1). Indigenous knowledge, on the other hand, has been framed in binary opposition to "scientific," "Western," "Eurocentric," or "modern" knowledge. Eurocentric thinkers have tended to dismiss Indigenous knowledge in the same way they dismissed any socio-political cultural life they did not understand. They found it to be unsystematic and incapable of meeting the productivity needs of the modern world (Battiste, 2005, p. 2). This is not to suggest that everyone within higher education exclusively subscribes to strictly Western paradigms and Western forms of learning and knowledge. There has been significant work done within many areas of academic scholarship to change these paradigms; in particular through feminist studies, critical pedagogy, critical theory, LGBT studies, and American Indian studies. I am suggesting, however that this is a tendency within Western academia and certainly still exists today, often unchallenged.

Western cultural paradigms and values have crept into every corner of the globe, bringing along American values, tastes, esthetic, and epistemologies, all of which are forms of Western hegemony. Huntington (1996) illustrates Western dominance and hegemony:

> Western, and more specifically American, popular culture is enveloping the world: American food, clothing, pop music, movies, and consumer goods are more and more enthusiastically embraced by people on every continent. ...the West has led the world to modern society, but that as people in other civilizations modernize they also Westernize, abandoning their traditional values, institutions, and customs and adopting those that prevail in the West. Both these project the image of an emerging homogeneous, universally Western world (p. 28)

Western epistemologies tend to support the notion that everything can be commodified, including activities, knowledge, and social relationships (Bowers, 2000, p. 74). American cultural paradigms tend to view human beings, cultures, and the natural world exclusively through the filter of their commodity value. Therefore, nearly everything in the West is reduced to its value in the marketplace (Welton, 1995). Bowers (2005) suggests the West spreads root cultural metaphors, along with economic and technological globalization. These root metaphors include thinking of everything, including plants and animals, as mechanistic in nature. Another cultural metaphor is the notion of anthropocentrism, that the environment is a resource for humans. "Progress" is another root metaphor that refers to change being something which helps move a culture forward by including more Western conveniences. The last metaphor is "economism," reducing activities, relationships, and products down to a market value (pp. 11-12).

Another form of Western hegemony is the insistence that Western culture is the universal standard, including demanding that English should be the universally standard language. The problem is that this push towards Western standardization has resulted in languages other than English being lost at a rapid rate. Language disappearance is often due to political forces. This means situations requiring people to speak English or a more "common" language than their native languages are more frequent. Approximately 80% of American Indian languages have been lost. Nearly 50% of the world's languages are endangered (Cantoni, 2007, p. vii). As Harjo and Bird (1997) proclaim, "But to speak, at whatever the cost, is to become empowered rather than victimized by destruction. In our tribal cultures, the power of language to heal, to regenerate, and to create is understood" (p. 21). Loss of language and culture is again a form of colonization and hegemony against Indigenous peoples. Yet English continues to become the universally standard language. The widespread usage of the Internet and computer technologies has made English even more prominent because most software programs and websites are written in English. Anyone who is a non-English speaker is forced to either learn English or suffer the consequences (Dyson & Underwood, 2006, pp. 64-66). People with rich linguistic and cultural traditions of the world are forced to abandon their languages and cultural values to engage with computer technology, specifically the Internet (Gordon, 2009). Master (1998) explains, "The negative aspect of the dominance of English lies in the extent to which it denies access, guarding the status quo and maintaining existing power structures" (p. 717). Along with most Internet and computer technologies being written in English is the implied spread of Western values. Technology is not neutral, but instead promotes Euro-American values (McLoughlin, 1999, p. 236). This type of hegemony means non-European, non-American people have to basically unlearn their own culture and assimilate different cultural values, a different language, and a different way of learning. Jiang (2011) notes that English cultural hegemony has already spread into China and Chinese life. There has been a quick permeation, which has had a direct influence on Chinese culture, ideology, and life (p. 194).

While it may not on the surface be a logical jump to include the influence of Christianity as a form of Western hegemony, I feel it bears exploring in this discussion. Underneath much of the cultural dominance of Western hegemony is the influence of Christianity on U.S. cultural values. The legality of the Church of Santo Daime and their ability to legally use ayahuasca is an example. According to Kivel (2013), "I define Christian hegemony as the everyday, systematic set of Christian values, individuals and institutions that dominate all aspects of U.S. society. Nothing is unaffected" (p. 3). Christian hegemony, therefore, is a worldview that works underneath the surface in American culture certainly, as part of Western hegemony.

The pervasive influence of Christianity on U.S. institutions can be specifically seen in accepted esthetics: laws pertaining to sexuality, morality, "foul language," birth control, women's rights, gay marriage, drug use, questions surrounding what constitutes an actual religion, and a myriad of other issues in everyday life in the United States. I am not arguing that all aspects of Christianity are necessarily wrong, nor that there is one set of Christians who all believe the same thing. That would be ridiculous. We can, however, look at the pervasive influence of Christianity as a form of hegemony, as an overt and covert influence in American culture and values. Kivel (2013) offers insights into Christian hegemony in the following way:

> Buried even deeper than policies and actions of institutions there seems to be a dominant Christian worldview that has shaped and skewed Western culture so profoundly that it is difficult to delineate fully. We have words for sexism, racism, and economic inequality, but what would we call the underlying, often hidden power of Christianity: Christianism? Christian dominance? Christian supremacy? (p. 2)

COLONIZATION

Colonization is another damaging force of oppression, but different than hegemony. Colonization is all about one more powerful group taking over another people. Colonizers may use hegemonic tactics to take over, but colonization is a different form of domination. Yellow Bird (2005) defined colonization as "referring to both the formal and informal methods (behaviors, ideologies, institutions, policies, and economies) that maintain the subjugation or exploitation of Indigenous peoples, lands, and resources. Colonizers engage in this process because it allows them to maintain and/or expand their social, political, and economic power" (p. 2). Fanon (1994) explains the depths of colonization in clear terms:

> Colonial domination, because it is total and tends to be over-simplified, very soon manages to disrupt in spectacular fashion the cultural life of conquered people. This cultural obliteration is made possible by the negation of natural reality, by new legal relations introduced by the occupying power, by the banishment of the natives and their customs to outlying districts by colonial society, by expropriation, and the systemic enslaving of men and women. (p. 45)

To explore colonization, I want to look at the colonization of American Indians. Taking American Indian lands, and in the process displacing people, is colonization. The Indian Removal Act of 1830, the Dawes Act, the Indian Reorganization Act, and other regressive anti-Indian acts are all forms of colonization. Forcing American Indian and Native Canadian children into boarding schools and taking away their language and religion is colonization. Forcing American Indians to sign treaties, only to break them, is colonization. Deloria and Lytle (1983) sum up American Indian colonization: "Indians have discovered that far too often legal doctrines purported to ensure their political and treaty rights are used to confiscate their property, deny their civil rights, and deprive them of their benefits that accrue with United States citizenship" (p. 95). These examples from Fanon, as well as Deloria and Lytle, give clear examples of colonization.

CONCLUSION

Hegemony works covertly, therefore it is often difficult to see, to understand, and to notice. Therefore, my goal in this chapter was to provide real world examples of hegemony and Western hegemony in action.

My larger goal is for you to clearly notice hegemony at play in your life, through your own hidden assumptions, and to then potentially understand its grip and influence on your life. From there, hopefully, we all can make choices to move away from hegemonic forces and liberate ourselves from the enslavement of this toxic form of power and domination.

Within the context of this book and my research, I want to explore and discuss hegemony in real-world terms. Throughout my doctoral research, my own criticism of academia is that concepts such as hegemony are discussed in an overly complicated and esoteric manner, so that the concepts become more and more abstract, and in the process less and less real and concrete. Almost as if some of the academic elite want to run from the visceral-level impact of the traps of hegemony, or deny the heartbreak and emotionally damaging component of hegemony's influences. Or, complicate issues related to hegemony so much that combatting hegemony becomes purely an intellectual exercise and not something real which we can all struggle against in the real world.

CHAPTER 3: Presentation of Research Interviews and Questionnaire Comments

You hold us through the night
You hold us through the night
Grandmother, you
You fill our hearts with joy
You fill our hearts with joy
Grandmother ayahuasca
You hold us close through the night
Healing us, Teaching us
Hold on, hold on as the waves move us through the night
Ayahuasca, we love you
Ayahuasca, we love you
Gratitude for this moment
Gratitude for your blessings.
(Ayahuasca ceremony healing song, used by permission from the Anonymous Ceremony Leader)

This chapter presents the data from the five steps of my research process. The first step was a short-qualitative interview pilot study in which people who have worked with ayahuasca were interviewed. Step 2: A quantitative scaled questionnaire pilot study was administered to participants around the world. Step 3: After changing the scaled questionnaire based on the data from both the qualitative and quantitative pilot studies and feedback from my dissertation committee, a revised scaled questionnaire was administered to a different set of participants. Step 4: Additional short qualitative interviews were conducted. Step Five: Several in-depth qualitative interviews were accomplished with an anonymous ayahuasca ceremony leader.

The working hypothesis throughout my research, that the ayahuasca experience might be an antidote to Western hegemony, was admittedly from the beginning a complex one. Both topics, the ayahuasca experience and the concept of hegemony, are not easy to understand. Hegemony tends to be invisible and hard to identify. The ayahuasca experience turns out to be similar to hegemony, in that it is hard to pin down, hard to understand, and manifests differently to different people.

Raw Interview Data

I am including the raw data from my interviews and also from the comments from participants in the online-scaled questionnaire. I wanted to include the unedited data so you could get a clearer picture of how interview participants discussed the ayahuasca experience in their own words and often in a raw mananer.

The process I followed to code, or organize, the interview data, was to first transcribe the interviews. Then I printed out the interviews in hard copy form to work with. Next, I read through each interview and when I noticed any participant comment (otherwise known as data) struck me as interesting, significant to my study, or relavent in any way, I would circle the word, phrase, or paragraph, and cut this chunk out and paste into a master document. The next step was to then organize these phrases and paragraphs thematically, so that I could start to look for patterns in my data related to ayahuasca and hegemony. My last step, after organizing the data, was to then break these anti-hegemonic concepts into themes. These themes are noted in the following chapter and organized as the five antidotal movements away from Western hegemony.

Data From Interviews

The data in this section contains my second pass at looking at the data and putting the phrases, sentences and words into 9 broad categories. To reiterate, the words and phrases listed here are direct quotes from participants and have not been edited in any way.

Theme 1: Self transformation/self healing /Personal meaning

-Self learning

- It's all about self learning
- The medicine reminds me to be a better person and what is important to me
- I get a sense of calm from the medicine and feel like my life is back on track
- I've seen people shed ignorant belief systems and grow and blossom
- I've met people who were healed by ayahuasca emotionally and spirituality
- It reemphasized what I already believed
- Deep connection to soul with light has helped me overcome those issues I struggled with
- I was in a mild depressive state and anxiety and it helped me
- Brought up childhood fears and trauma for me to face and deal with
- Catalyst for change
- I was unprepared for the changes
- The fear of being opened up in such a raw state
- Increased my desire to spend more time on my creative expressions
- This tool helped reclaim some things that were lost or to rectify some things within myself
- Aware of old dysfunctional patterns, relationships that didn't work
- I'm less likely to get hooked into rage and anger
- It's more of an awareness of an internal filing system where memories that are either painful or joyful get fragmented and then the process works to reorganize them or restructure them
- It gives me new ways of looking at old experiences
- Feeling of deep peace and love
- Clarity around what is important and what is not
- Basic healing
- It's helped me understand myself, let go of things I needed to let go of, personality, thought patterns, lifestyles
- Healing traumas from the past
- Old patterns being healed
- Awareness shifted
- More compassionate and less judgmental
- It was like therapy, but much deeper
- I saw how stuck I was
- Found peace
- Doing the hard work on yourself and examining your own shit, and bringing it forward into the world
- I have come to peace with certain things about being a woman, things that felt stuck before
- Self love from the ayahuasca, which has been a huge part of the process for me

-It was a healing process
-It has helped me act with more integrity at my job.
-Instead of hooking into drama I try to step back more
-Deep level change
-It opens you up
-It's a healing path
-Letting go
-Less drama
-Smashes your ego
-Learned about myself and my traumas in my life, my family heritage, my ancestral lineage
-I've learned what it means to be a human on earth
-I've learned I do not have to inherit my families' issues
-I have changed how I treat self, others, the way I behave, and the person that I am
-It re-emphasized my values
-Your values, priorities, and worlds are different after
-I used to smoke a lot of pot, but then gave it up after the medicine
-The medicine is very empowering and made me feel more capable doing more with my life

Theme 2: Others, community, positioning self as community member, changes in relating to others

-Everyone is coming to ceremony and has their own set of concerns, problems, issues or past, hurt and wounds and once you see that you realize we are all in this together
-It has taught me a great reverence for other people in general
-I have a deeper relationship with what it means to pray in community
-Empathy for others
-Greater awareness of how we interact with the people in the world
-More aware of what others are going through
-More empathy
-Even though we are all different on the outside, inside we are all the same and all deal with the same stuff
-Family was more important
-Greater sense of responsibility for the world
-Supporting people in my spiritual community is now a priority
-Connected deeply with people and the medicine

-The medicine put me more in tune with how people work, see deeper into people
-I'm more patient with people
-Feeling others suffering
-To hold myself to a higher standard and do right by people
-I have the desire to give back to others
-Caring for others and giving what you can is more important and more rewarding
-It showed me a lot about how I interact with people
-I think the medicine will heal my family
-Seeing greater beauty in people
-I just try to do things to help other people
-We are the people we have been waiting for

Theme 3: Plants, nature, Mother Nature, Plant Teachers, environmental awareness and appreciation

-Connecting with plant and animal spirits directly
-I'm much more sympathetic about what is going on with Mother Earth
-It's sad to see the earth be destroyed
-I make decisions about what I purchase, so that I live my life and do so more in accord with the environment and recycling
-These ceremonies connect us back to nature, to the natural world, because we are so removed from it
-Before ayahuassca I never viewed plants as sentient beings that I could communicate with or that had an independent consciousness
-Remorse for the rain forest
-You have to let go when you walk with the plants
-Working with ayahuasca means a commitment to the plants
-Awareness of how the earth is being destroyed
-I feel a connection with plants so much
-The plants will teach you
-I made a commitment to the plants
-Commitment to the medicine
-I have learned about how the plant works, not that I even understand 1% of how it works
-The sentience of the plant medicine
-Sentient, intelligent force in the plant medicine
-Awe and reverence for nature

-When you connect with the plants you disconnect from greed, jealousy and anger
-We are supposed to be one with Mother Earth and plants, and everything. Until we walk that walk and let the plants teach us and help us understand that again, we are separate

Theme 4: Materialism/commodification/career

-The work I do now is important enough and makes me happy to be doing it and that has a greater value to me than making more money
-I live simply and don't have a lot of stuff, nor do I want a lot of stuff
-Before the medicine I thought I always had to have like this career and a lot of money
- I think once I started working with the medicine I realized that the whole way of thinking was not where I needed to be (being career focused and making more money)
-Before I was more likely to get comfort from material goods, now it doesn't matter
-I look at how I spent my money differently
-Ayahuasca helped me relating to my profession and financial situation
-I want to have a comfortable life, but for others to have that too
-People associated with the medicine path have the approach to living life in a light, unattached way regarding belongings
-Anecdotally, it seems that people who use medicine tend to be less materialistically attached
-It changed my focus to be more of a healer and not just a corporate slave
-Lost the drive to make more money and get a better position at the company
-Removed material bonds—because they weigh you down

Theme 5: Criticality: social, political, oppression and awareness—social awareness versus political awareness

-I have a different notion of what an ideal politician would act and be like
-If politicians used ayahuasca they would care less about ego and power
-It makes you more sensitive and more aware of what is going on in the world. And that doesn't go away. It has a lasting effect.
-I have found that over time I am much more involved and intrigued by what is happening my immediate area, politically, much more than before the

medicine
-Before the medicine I was thinking of politics on a more worldly scale, but now it's more about my immediate surroundings. With the medicine I've realized there is not a whole lot I can accomplish in a worldly way, but from a local place I can bring about change and effect people. I'm also just more interested in what is happening locally
-It has helped me to see a broader scope, to be more critical, discerning, understanding whether local politics or people arguing
-Christianity messed up Indigenous peoples
-The ceremonies have made me skeptical and critical of Western medicines
-I guess I'm apolitical now
-Politically, I've given up on politics
-I ignore politics because it is so screwed up
-More socially aware, but I don't follow what is going on
-More socially aware of the importance of the rainforest
-You see injustices more and the way the status quo has set up the world
-After ayahuasca some people become more politically active or want to become healers
-I'm apathetic to politics
-You feel from ayahuasca you have the support to be courageous in life and stop injustice
-The medicine made my commitment to social justice and caring for people stronger
-Put me in touch with oppression
-I felt a strong sense of empathy of the effects of oppression and exploitation
-Aware of what is' like when people take advantage of others for their resources
-It teaches you to hold your own and not care what people think
-The whole political scheme is dysfunctional. All these egos
-There's no love in politics
-Politicians are destroying our lives and destroying Pachamama, and destroying everything

Theme 6: Experiences during ayahuasca ceremonies/the process

-All of my ayahuasca experiences have been so different
-There are some really beautiful visions with the medicine; it can be idealistic
-There's a physical discomfort and an emotional uncomfortableness, but on the other side I feel free

-It was like a series of movies about my life and each time I do it, it adds another chapter to the plot
-There is always so much personalization to the experiences that I hear when others share about it too
-It's a physical ordeal; it's very challenging
-There's a lot of after thought processing
-I saw that in some ways I'm just a cog in a wheel
-After ceremony there was a sense of loneliness and isolation
-Medicine gets at gets at root of people's problems, healing physical, emotional and spiritual bodies
-The medicine shows how wrong headed it is to not use natural based remedies for simple things
-It's not recreational
-It's a utopia
-It can fade away
-I've seen crazy miracles
-I felt the cords being cut away from people attacking me
-It is both more connecting and isolating
-Sublime spirits teach shamans the mystic nature and the workings of the plant selves
-It's medicine
-Ayahuasca made it clear to me that the only technology you really need is ancient technology built into our brains, hearts, plants and the universe
-We haven't begun to tap into the mechanics of this ancient technology
-It's a plant and a beautiful medicine that heals people, heals bodies, heals interpersonal relationships and societal relationships
-Western medicine doesn't do this
-Medicine can enlighten you
-Wisdom of the medicine
-Ayahuasca is very inclusive; it can co-exist
-Spirit came to me
-An angel touched me and told me about my third eye and the importance of my pineal gland
-I learned what it meant to pray
-Reconnecting to sprit
-Spiritual opening

Theme 7: Random, miscellaneous comments

-Judeo-Christianity subverting Indigenous traditions
-Life puts you into a position where you are a puppet
-I don't think the experience has changed my basic morals or philosophical outlook
-It's a lifetime experience and a lifetime devotion, not a recreational thing
-When it comes down to it, things really don't matter so much
-Critical of the drug laws by the government making ayahuasca illegal
-There's my will and then there's the medicine's will
-You are like a puppet
-As you dedicate more of your life to this path, you end up feeling a little more alien
-All psychedelics can be a force of social change. That's why LSD was made illegal
-I see a lot of Western people treat ayahuasca like LSD, and psychonauts treating it as a journey through the mind and nothing more.
-Judeo Christianity is an oppressive force that tries to subvert indigenous traditions

EXCERPTS FROM THE INTERVIEWS WITH THE ANONYMOUS CEREMONY LEADER

What follows are several of the interview questions I asked an anonymous ceremony leader during four interview sessions. I did not include the raw data here because parts of the interviews are used in other places in this book. Some of the interviews contained data I did not find applicable to my study or the interviews contained information that was repetitive, such as stories told more than once. These interviews were instructive to my study, however, as the anonymous ceremony leader, without prompting, discussed many issues related to Western hegemony. It was also instructive to my study to talk to someone over a series of interviews about ayahuasca who could also share resources with me, such as song lyrics and books and articles to read.

What was your motivation for going to an ayahuasca ceremony?

I was dragged into it. I thought it would be a bunch of hippies, using hallucinogens, being stupid, dumb, acting goofy, but the people (mostly South Americans) were very serious, kind, and very committed to working with ayahuasca. It was the most down-to-earth spiritual community I had experienced. And I was impressed by the inner strength of the people to stay awake most of the night and work so hard.

How did you go from being a participant to a ceremony leader?

I worked with the medicine for a many years, and eventually traveled with a group of 20 people from South America to participate in an immersion program in Peru. While I was there, I was probably the least likely to lead ceremonies. However, the ayahuasqueros basically forced me to bring medicine home and work with it. I went from being intimidated by ayahuasca to seeing its facility to make a difference and be healing for people. A huge amount of work goes into learning about ayahuasca. It takes decades to start to understand the process.

How many times have you participated in ayahuasca ceremonies?

Easily more than 700 times.

Did participating in ceremonies change your relationship to nature and people?

There have been a lot of shifts. No epiphany, but changes grounded in experience. I went from not having consciousness of plants to seeing animals as sentient, viscerally, experientially, and cognitively. When you work with ayahuasca, there are a myriad of experiences that may happen, and it's different every time. It makes you wonder. It quickly becomes clear that the plant has consciousness. Ayahuasca taught me to relate to nature and plants as spirits, teachers, healers, and relatives. I never learned that from my family of origin, culture, education, or other spiritual path.

Do you think it's been healing for others?

It's variable. But yes, I think it's helped people with depression, anxiety, to feel good with their life. It has psychotherapeutic effects. If people come to ceremony one or two times, there is not much change, they are more like spiritual tourists. But if you have an intense focus, you get something.

Some people get stuck in narcissism. They think they "know" things, but it's spiritual arrogance. The medicine is so powerful that after drinking it, a person might think they are unique, a special person. It can inflate ego, but then it deflates ego.

Do you think it's been healing for you?

Yes. It has helped me with social anxiety. Sitting in ceremonies has challenged my American notion of personal space, and that I am so special and important and at the center of the universe. I think ayahuasca has given me a more mature outlook on life and helped me to become aware of the suffering others are going through.

Will you continue to lead ceremonies?

It has been part of my life for more than 20 years. There was a time when it was seen as illegal and scrutinized, but now not so much.

Has leading ceremonies changed your views of social justice?

It's made me aware of pain, more sensitive to forms of oppression, sexual abuse. Going to Peru made me more aware of clearcutting [the Amazon Rainforest] and environmental injustice. Before, I understood that intellectually. Plants are powerful and should be protected. I have become more sensitive to and appreciative of nature wherever I go.

Little by little, we realize what we are told by the outside world is bullshit. The idea of Manifest Destiny, that we are the center of the world and you can do whatever you want, none of those things are sustainable and all cause problems.

What are the major things the medicine has taught you?

Ceremonies are a challenge. You have to breathe through the roller coaster. It has taught me more compassion, to be less judgmental, more open. I used to be bothered by people fidgeting, making noise, and being inappropriate. Now I see the service in it.

Ceremony gives personal meaning to people's lives; it shapes and gives meaning. Some people have no sense of purpose. They are searching, but they don't go deep on any path. They feel incomplete, which creates depression and lack of meaning. Participating in ceremonies helps to frame life and gives it meaning and purpose.

Has leading ceremonies changed your political views?

I think it has changed my view to more right-seeing – through sitting, concentrating, and being open, I see politics more clearly. Before, I was left-identified. Now I am more problem-solving-identified. I am more aware of corruption. Before, I didn't think it affected me. Now I am more likely to be locally active, like supporting the local organic meat market. I see myself in the community more.

I think the Indigenous view of plant medicines is it that the medicine shows you the way things really are. How do we reconcile what a Western mind might call a "hallucination" versus seeing things the way they are?

That only points to one chunk of what happens in an ayahuasca ceremony. One chunk might be a vision or hallucination, you might have a physical sensation, or an inner dialogue or you may be more daydreamy, in more of a relaxed setting.

When you talk about a vision, one of the ways of the language of medicine is through metaphor and that's true in a lot of indigenous healing practices is that we live in that level of experience; it's a metaphor. Visions of snakes coming from the sky, for example, is a common representation of ayahuasca itself that could mean a lot of different things.

It isn't literal that we are in this hallucination and there is a literal "seeing things as they are." It could be that the metaphor is how things are. We don't see ourselves how we really are. Everything is illusory. We know that the chair looks solid, but it's not really solid, it's made of space on a cellular level. The wall looks solid, but if we peel off the drywall, there is actual space behind it. Things are not unchanging.

Part of it is laziness of the Western mind or the people who are tourists who don't come and really work with ayahuasca. First cut may be this big thing: "This eagle came to me and told me I'm a healer." That's bullshit, that's ego mind. But if you looked at a vision, people see colors, fields of colors, stuff like that that. That may be how things are. There is energy floating by and it does have color. It's hard to say there is one type of vision.

Some of that is the purging of the self, of old limiting beliefs, of old views of reality, old things that are stuck in our cell memory. So it's hard to know. Some people claim when people see scary things, it's a detoxification of the liver. I don't know if that true; I'm not a doctor. Some of the things there may be a logical explanation for, but it could be real. We don't really know.

I'm concerned that people walk away in a stronger place where things make more sense in the morning or a week or month or year from know. That's what I'm concerned about. I'm not concerned with the vision and people grasping on to a vision. Every time you do ayahuasca, it's a different experience. It's like a Tibetan sand painting; once it's over it's over, it's beautiful and it's done. Some if it is people being able to relate to themselves as beautiful, to see inner beauty and to see outer beauty. How those work together. A person can't recognize external beauty without seeing inner beauty, or inner beauty without external beauty. To have the experience of self in that way again ties to metaphor, where we don't know.

This is like any high-level skill or understanding. You don't go once and think you know it all. You don't go to one session of a Master's degree class or Ph.D. class and think you have the whole thing mastered. This is a fairly complicated philosophy and takes a lot of study and a lot of work and a lot of application to understand. It isn't simple.

How do you think it affects your daily life?

There's a cumulative effect of feeling good, OK in my body and OK in my skin. There's an expansion in capacity to care for other people and concern for other people other than myself. That's a change. For the good and bad of it, the people you do ceremony with become your family. If you have a crazy aunt or whatever, they are part of the family. It becomes a big extended family and big responsibility. So that's part of my daily life, people who come to ceremony.

Maybe it's just me, but I try to hold myself to a standard and bring it into my neighborhood and my community to the best of my ability. It's never that far away from the ceremony, the ayahuasca and me. Grandmother Ayahuasca is part of my daily life.

Qualitative Scaled Questionnaire Comments

One of my methods of data collection was to conduct a scaled survey. During one of the last phases of my research, I re-wrote the survey and also added a field for survey participants to add any comments they wanted to make about ayahuasca, ayahuasca ceremonies, or anything else. My hope was that this would give more opportunity for people in an anonymous setting to express their feelings and thoughts openly about ayahuasca and the ayahuasca experience. The data presented a wide range of comments, from someone commenting that ayahuasca is "God in a glass" to someone criticizing the research questions for being too specific. Twenty-nine out of 44 questionnaire participants left comments. I have included all of the comments from participants. I am including the comments participants' wrote exactly as they were sent to me. Since this was the precise manner the comments were sent to me, I did not feel it was appropriate to edit them, or change them in any way. Therefore, the raw data is included for you to read and draw your own interpretations about these comments.

1. *I strongly respect and I'm aware of the sacred nature of the plant teachers/healers. I believe that they can help shift consciousness on a planetary level, to make us more aware of others and the planet, and our role and place in the human evolution.*
1/18/2015 11:42 AM

2. *I am so grateful for the ceremony I experienced, and the ceremony leader's guidance through it. It expanded my awareness in a way I never thought possible.*
1/17/2015 9:13 PM

3. *While I've always had a strong desire for community connection, support, and intention to improve it, I think the medicine and ceremony have helped me internalize the experience that love and compassion are the foundation for these connections. I can participate and play a part in improving my community, but the true connection occurs through love and compassion and subsequently non-judgment. I think ayahuasca and the ayahuasca community has helped me feel and express compassion and empathy in a more natural, authentic way.*
1/17/2015 8:23 PM

4. *Aya for me has helped me address the critical imbalances within my self and ego. Through Aya ceremony, I have been able to gain insight into these issues and also have grown my ability to focus on them in a productive and meaningful way. I feel more connected with myself and with nature and the total environment*

as a result of my experiences with Aya. My relationships with my friends and community have also improved.
1/17/2015 12:19 PM

5. I find ayahuasca ceremony to be a wonderful opportunity to focus inward and utilize my own tools for self-care. I am concerned about women's safety as traveling females go to South America for ayahuasca. I don't think ayahuasca can teach me anything I can't learn in other ways. I just prefer ayahuasca because it's a meditation as well as a detox. I can do without all the psychedelic talk surrounding the medicine and like to work with shamen who are humble and who support equality for women.
1/15/2015 9:57 PM

6. The framing of this survey could lead one to believe that ayahuasca did not have much of an effect on me, which is not the case of my experience at all. My experience with ayahuasca simply affirmed the belief systems I already had going into it. It revealed itself as a life tool I can use to expand on my own understanding of nature, and how our political systems and social structures can corrupt an individual and keep him/her from living harmoniously with plant and animal spirits. Ayahuasca has enlightened my understanding of certain family members and their struggle to move forward with their own lives (i.e. why they have always seemed rather stunted in their spiritual understanding of the world.) I do not recommend that others use ayahuasca, but I think that those who are brave enough to do so walk away from it feeling empowered and connected to the universal consciousness.
1/14/2015 6:10 PM

8. Ayahuasca is a safe and effective medicine to help heal the mind and body. It should be available to everyone who is in need of healing. Ayahuasca has spiritual benefits as well. People that have been healed with ayahuasca are happier, healthier, have better relationships, and feel that their life has purpose.
1/13/2015 8:00 AM

9. It's difficult convey how significantly changed I am through my ayahuasca experiences if I stick only to the questions in this survey. Certainly some of my social and political behaviors have been influenced. But the most profound changes have been more deeply personal. I have been introduced to myself, my fears and flaws, but also my beauty and sense of comfort and satisfaction with who I am. I have done a fair amount of therapy and self improvement, taken depression medications to deal with depression, family issues and cultural issues related to being a woman. None have amounted to any really lasting change in how I relate to myself or to my

community at large. Finally, at the midpoint in my life, I moved past a being stuck in my pre-adolescence and relate to myself as an adult woman with full ownership and responsibility for who I am in the world. It's not that I'm more politically active, as a hobby to keep myself busy. It's that I feel a sense of ownership and responsibility for who I am in society.

Also, ayahuasca has shown me how things and people are all connected and influence one another. The risk associated with me being uninvolved, self-involved or negatively involved in community is too great. This is how the things noted in the survey are impacted by my ayahuasca experiences.
12/30/2014 10:31 AM

10. After experiencing ayahuasca, the biggest effect is that I'm more aware of my spiritual life, the power of self-healing psychological ills, the power that music has in this, and the effect that I can have in this way towards others. Real connection with others and with the community is more important, although I was mostly buying local when possible before as well. After a number of Ayahuasca experiences, live music is more powerful and attractive, but not all types--personal, acoustic, spiritual performances appeal more than more commercial shows--and mass media has less appeal, although I have always been more attracted books and reading than television newscasts, for example.
12/28/2014 9:13 PM

11. Transformed my life, helped me re-evaluate everything. It shows you what you should do, it's not the remedy.
12/20/2014 12:44 AM

12. The primary reason I started to use Ayahuasca was for healing work- History of sexual abuse/incest, which led to addictions. I have been drinking for 8 years now and am learning how to better function as a compassion human being. I realized the world needs healing and ayahuasca was a very positive and beneficial way to begin. I feel blessed and have much gratitude to the plant spirits and to those who work with the plants.
12/19/2014 3:54 PM

13. Hi researcher, Just some words on your survey from my experience. I think you´re making a division that does not exist. This before/after divide may lead to a very obvious narrative of the person who started to believe in forest souls and be against GMO's after taking ayahuasca and sharing shamanic beliefs and so on. Why not focus on the type of political consciousness that having ayahuasca may

enable and whether it is put to work or not. From my experience, it may bring lots of environmental consciousness but this does not match with political consciousness/practice/action at all. After taking part in some ayahuasqueiros groups I actually thought they were way too closed/alienated to criticize society as a whole and so on, as the main concerns were on seeking spiritual cleanse and pursue a more holy path in daily life... Said that, I do often feel that ayahuasca groups are even conservative or could be related to a sort of liberal politics... I think the break with western beliefs on, for instance, medicine or health treatment, could be enacted as a political contest, though I would not put things in these terms.

Sometimes sociologists/anthropologists are struggling at the institutional level for recognition of rights of ayahuasca groups and the right to be there, prepare, gathering and so on, what may be deemed as a political activity, but that is not the case for the average consumer in the countryside of Germany or Spain that eventually have the tea with a pass-by shaman. Anyway, I think you could work a bit more on your premises/hypothesis and hope my words not being so uncomfortable. I actually think in a way that ayahuasca does provide you with a consciousness about people and environment. In practical terms, however, it is not put to work, or, at least not enough let's say, to make a critique on neoliberal politics.

So why? Besides struggles for legalisation of use and rituals etc, and sometimes some philanthropic, popular action in the community where the group is settle, how the ayahuasca community is fighting and really providing a counter-narrative? Are they? I think I´m sharing this due my disappointment with some groups and the neglected ideological effects of ayahuasca on people. It could be revolutionary but it is not. My best wishes for your research.
12/13/2014 12:31 PM

14. Ayahuasca changed my life. I thought I was already open minded, but now feel much more so. It has made me feel more connected to people, animals and nature. I think I am more empathetic now.
12/13/2014 11:41 AM

15. Aya taught me how to be a better human being, not to be afraid of death, feel more compassion especially toward family members. It changed my diet and my habits. I became prolife with respect to my own life choices. It taught me to respect and cherish all life. It showed me God and history of creation. It opened my heart chakra. It made me to be honest with myself. It showed me how to change my family's karma.
12/13/2014 11:11 AM

16. Before ayahuasca I was unaware that we have alien heritage now I am convinced we have alien heritage.
12/13/2014 11:02 AM

17. God in a glass.
12/13/2014 10:54 AM

18. I was total skeptical before to try Ayahuasca, I had my hopes and faith lost, I even started to lose my religion and didn't believe in anything else, because being a good person and aware of many things in this world, everything went bad and painful in my life. Ayahuasca gave me back hopes, taught me that things happen for a reason and I should believe, because we create what we believe. My depression continues in nowadays but is comforting to know that this life is not all.
12/13/2014 10:44 AM

19. I had a lot of these characteristics before I took ayahuasca, so having taken it, they didn't change a discernable amount. I have always had a strong connection to the Earth and fought for equality. I see it as a longer timeline, starting with me being a child who loved the woods and then a hardcore straight edge punk rocker with a political bent on up to the yoga teacher and astrologer I am now. All of these things served to give me a more universal and non-judgmental mindset and a desire to heal and help this world. The ayahuasca appeared in my life when it was needed to kick start some faster evolution.
12/10/2014 6:07 PM

20. [These comments are in Portuguese.] A Ayahuasca me ajudou muito em vários fatores: 1 - Deixei de comer carne, tomar refrigerantes, bebidas com álcool. 2 - Amor pela natureza, tendo uma vida mais natural, com banhos de rios e cachoeiras. 3 - Amor e respeito pelos meus familiares e animais. 4 - Tomar decisões acertadas. 5- Conexão com o mundo espiritual. Aprendi a rezar e agradecer ao universo. (Translated to English as: Ayahuasca helped me on several factors : 1 - I stopped eating meat , taking soft drinks, drinks with alcohol. 2 - Love for nature, and a more natural life, with baths in rivers and waterfalls. 3 - Love and respect for my family and animals. 4 - Taking decisions. 5- connection with the spirit world. I learned to pray and thank the universe.)
12/3/2014 3:20 PM

21. After taking Ayahuasca I feel less inclined to drink alcohol. I have started meditating, eating healthier and taken steps to build a healthier and happier life. I feel a greater sense of connectedness with everything and everyone around me.

12/2/2014 9:32 AM

22. After taking Ayahuasca I can feel more clarity in my brain. After taking Ayahuasca I became a better person in all aspects. After taking Ayahuasca I LOVE my self much more. After taking Ayahuasca I make peace with in me and myself. After taking Ayahuasca I can feel the eternal universal unconditional LOVE. After taking Ayahuasca I realize we all are shamans. After taking AYAHUASCA I realize superstition does not exist. After taking Ayahuasca I interact much more with my inner child. After taking Ayahuasca I can feel UNITY, no separation. After taking Ayahuasca I realizer competition is supports separation. After taking Ayahuasca I realisze the infinito (and that I AM...).

After taking Ayahuasca I feel we are everything and nothing. After taking Ayahuasca I lose fear. After taking Ayahuasca I realize I am much more than just this body that is only loaned for this short period we call life. After taking Ayahuasca I realize my path of this lifetime. After taking Ayahuasca I realize the powers we have to heal. After taking Ayahuasca I understand the LIGHT, PHOTONS, and how they work. After taking Ayahuasca I realize the message of the masters of LOVE. After taking Ayahuasca I understood the Alchemy of the body. After Ayahuasca I can feel my vibratory frequency is higher and it stay there higher and higher. After taking Ayahuasca I realize everything is subjective. After taking Ayahuasca my understanding of spirit is more understood. After taking Ayahuasca I can go on and on and on. I AM THAT, I AM.
12/2/2014 8:00 AM

23. Having never had any experiences with psychoactive herbs or medicines of any kind, Aya was a complete game changer for me. The most terrifying and intense experience of my life. So awakening, so interactive and experiential and so completely healing and loving. I am forever changed.
12/2/2014 2:27 AM

24. The possible cure to all the ills of mankind. I have participated in four ceremonies, having more profound visions than the next. It it is literally a life changing medicine. Good luck.
12/2/2014 1:03 AM

25. It helped me see myself for what and who I truly am. I enjoyed and learned a lot.
12/2/2014 12:08 AM

26. Before my experiences with ayahuasca in the Peruvian Amazon, I was already a very socially and consciously aware individual, so my feelings and sentiments weren't particularly altered. However talking with others taking part in the ayahuasca ceremonies, it was a wake up call for many who didn't see the world in such ways beforehand, painting a clearer picture of injustice and inequality in our world.
12/1/2014 1:11 PM

27. I wish I could have helped with this survey before it was created. Things are not more or less important to me now. Things now just are. Ayahuasca changed my relation to all that is on Earth by showing me how it doesn't really matter. The entire scope of the universe is so vast to me now, that I see it will all end, everything breaks, dies or is destroyed, and will someday be gone to us and us gone to it. It did fill me with a sense of true love, which has moved me to live life in a completely different way. I have a greater love for everyone because I now see that although it will end, we are all impermanent, and we have choice to act. So we can act from love or not from love, and no matter what we do, it's just part of a giant co-experience. I am more politically aware, but less angry about what I see.

I was very politically active when [Gov.]Scott Walker started making changes with Wisconsin, and went daily to protests. Now I feel that the best work I can do may not be from standing in a crowd of people in front of a news camera pointed the other way, but to act from love as much as possible, because it seems that nothing can change the world more than love. I care less about possessions and respect what I have more, but if I don't need it, I feel a need to get it to someone who will. I feel more compassionate about the world, animals, etc. and want to help. I'm more in the now and less in the past or future, but that makes it hard to move in any certain direction in a big way. Right now, I'm just contemplating my experiences with Ayahuasca, remaining inspired by them, and creating from them. I spend more time living one day at a time, and within that day, one hour at a time, doing what inspires, motivates and compels me.
12/1/2014 11:20 AM

28. I knew before taking aya there was another reality beside what we experience, but after experiencing it with aya it has profoundly changed the way I see the world, my priorities, and my ability to open my heart and feel love.
12/1/2014 10:11 AM

29. The main shift in my politics was one from a doomsday/conspiracy/catastrophe perception to one that embraced the possibility for change. With these new

possibilities I feel empowered to speak/ represent/ and act with greater capacity. As an artist I feel necessary to contribute to the community before personal expression. I also feel compelled to create and offer works that offer connection and transformation — before the ayahuasca experience I was putting on events like Hawaiian Rawk Fests — after offering song circles and Biodanza Workshops. I also feel that I shifted from resistance culture into a culture of positive social change. For example, I used to live in anarchist or arts collectives, but now I live in a community house centered around eco-art, organic gardening, and high vibrational living. In the greater sense Ayahuasca provided the template to refine my lifestyle and political action to one that embraces intercultural perspectives, transformational approaches, and compassion. Ayahuasca and the community involved with the medicine continue to be an infinite resource of inspirational and guidance for living life.
12/1/2014 9:08 AM

Conclusion

This chapter presented the data from all five steps of my research process. The thematically coded interview data was grouped into interview data presented a mix of data, some showing a potential connection between ayahuasca usage and changes in hegemonic themes. At the same time, some of the questions showed no connection, or data that were difficult or inconclusive. During my short interviews, I uncovered data that seemed to suggest a strong connection between ayahuasca usage and changes in Western hegemonic themes. During this step in the research, there were many participants who had used ayahuasca more than one hundred times. All of the data contained in this chapter from the scaled questionnaires, the interviews with the anonymous ceremony leader, and the short interviews all inform the findings from my study. I have included the data in mostly raw form so you can see for yourself the data about ayahuasca and read the unedited comments about ayahuasca and ayahuasca ceremonies. In particular, the unedited comments from participants in the scaled questionnaire are interesting and offer glimpses into the psyches of people who work with ayahuasca.

CHAPTER 4: The Five Antidotes to Western Hegemony Connected to Working with Ayahuasca

"When we drink ayahuasca we evolve and gain power and lucidity. Then we can create actions that take form in the world, and change the future and the past too. If there is some trauma in the past, for example, it can come up through ayahuasca, but then it can be healed. That's what ayahuasca is for."
(Peruvian ayahuasca master Guillermo Arevelo, in Heaven & Charing, 2006, p. 88)

This chapter summarizes all of the data from all five steps of the research process into themes related to Western hegemony and ayahuasca ceremony participants. Specifically, when the qualitative data were coded using thematic analysis, five antidotes to Western hegemony were revealed. This chapter also presents quantitative data to suggest that there is a connection between people working with ayahuasca more than 50 times and a movement away from Western hegemony. These changes can be found both in the qualitative and the quantitative data.

I am describing these as "movements" away from a hegemonic structure towards an antidote because I feel it more accurately depicts what the data have suggested: that the ayahuasca experience and its unique form of challenging hegemony is a process, oftentimes a lengthy process. The ayahuasca process may be abstract and not necessarily a Western form of additive knowledge over a period of time, or singular dramatic shifts at one time. However, the research data show clear evidence that over time, long-term ayahuasca users do show movements away from Western hegemonic structure towards an antidote because I feel it more accurately depicts what the data have suggested: that the ayahuasca experience and its unique form of challenging hegemony is a process, oftentimes a lengthy process. The ayahuasca process may be abstract and not necessarily a Western form of additive knowledge over a period of time, or singular dramatic shifts at one time. However, the research data show clear evidence that over time, long-term ayahuasca users do show movements away from Western hegemonic structures towards Indigenous-based antidotes. It is not realistic to think of the ayahuasca process as a miracle cure or a panacea of some sort. The notion of "movement" seems to imply a more organic change model as well — which more aligns with an Indigenous worldview.

As the ayahuasca ceremony leader suggests in one of his interviews,

> Little by little we learn to work with the medicine. Little by little we let go of what holds us back inside ourselves. Little by little the Grandmother [ayahuasca] helps to reveal that we are divine and we live in a divine world full of divine people and divine plants and animals. Ayahuasca mirrors back to us that the medicine is divine and we are divine.

For each of the five antidotes, I provide a brief definition and exploration of its related Western hegemonic structures, followed by a description of the potential antidote as it relates to the research data. I present direct quotes from interview participants that align with these antidotes. As part of my description and definitions, I draw from theories of Indigenous scholars to ground this exploration within an Indigenous worldview.

- **Antidote 1:** Movement from the personal trappings of Western hegemony towards self-determination.

- **Antidote 2:** Movement from individuality and "survival of the fittest" toward relationality and being kinship-focused.

- **Antidote 3:** Movement from anthropocentrism towards an anthropomorphic view of the natural world.

- **Antidote 4:** Movement from being materially and commodity focused towards meaning and purpose found outside of consumerism and commodification.

- **Antidote 5:** Movement from unconsciousness regarding political and social influences, towards criticality, or even rejection of these influences.

Age as a Factor in the Data Results

When I began to analyze the quantitative data, one of the questions I had was related to whether or not age was a factor in the answers given to the questions asked on the scaled questionnaire. I hypothesized that one's age could certainly be a major factor in one's hegemonic awareness, and perhaps this type of awareness is simply more prevalent in adults over 40 years of age, for instance. Furthermore, my assumption was that natural developmental life stages affect natural changes related to beliefs, attitudes, and possibly a shift in worldview might result in older ayahuasca ceremony participants reporting a movement away from hegemonic forces having nothing to do with the ayahuasca experience, but simply based on their own process of maturing. I also thought age could be a factor in the participants who have worked with ayahuasca more than 50 times simply because that volume of ayahuasca usage could possibly take someone 10 years, which would simply put them in an older age group.

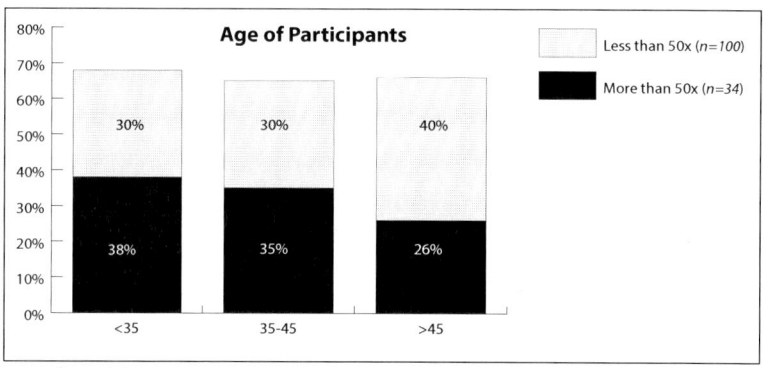

Age of participants.

When I re-configured the data to look at changes in ayahuasca users over 45 years of age compared to those below 45, the participants over the age of 45 are fairly evenly distributed among various age categories. The figure below, looking at the age of participants, seems to suggest that age simply is not a large factor in the quantitative data.

Gender as a Factor in the Data Results

In examining the data, I was also not sure if gender would play a role in skewing the results of the quantitative scaled questionnaire one way or another. One gender might be more likely to answer the questions one way or another, thus affecting the data. Figure 39 shows that the gender makeup of research participants is almost identical in the group who has worked with ayahuasca more than 50 times compared to the group who has worked with ayahuasca less than 50 times. As a result, gender does not appear to be a factor in changing quantitative data one way or another.

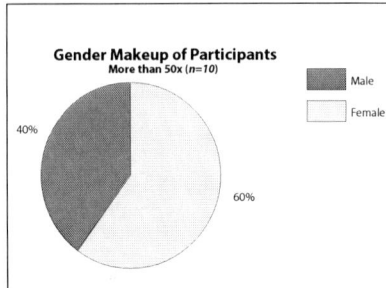 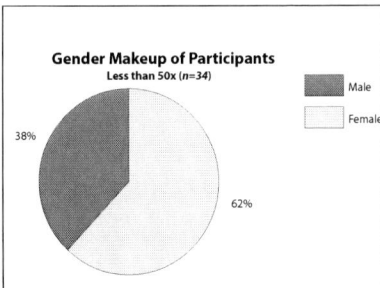

Comparision of gender of participants-qualitative data: More than 50x ayahuasca versus less than 50x ayahuasca.

Major Findings in the Data

Both the qualitative and quantitative research data suggest there is a movement or a change in people who experience ayahuasca. The changes appear to be greater in those who have worked with ayahuasca more than 50 times. One-hundred percent of the participants who had worked with ayahuasca more than 50 times spoke about changes related to each of the five antidotes. Samples from these interviews are contained in this chapter. The quantitative data also show a movement away from hegemonic structures. I reconfigured the data from the revised scaled questionnaire of those who have worked with ayahuasca more than 50 times. The reconfigured data show a larger antidotal movement in this group of participants than in the group of participants who have worked with ayahuasca less than 50 times. While the sample sizes to each step of my study were small, the data suggest that the five antidotes to Western hegemony are present in each method employed in the study.

Antidote 1:
Movement from the Personal Trappings of Western Hegemony Towards Self-Determination

This antidote and its movement suggests that the ayahuasca experience often assists participants in personal-level healing, which includes a transformation in personal meaning, healing trauma, regaining perspective on their lives, feeling more connected to their personal purpose, and assisting in change from the "inside out."

Western Hegemonic Structure

Western hegemony preys on people in the arena of personal beliefs and attitudes. Western hegemony and its force towards commodification push the notion that individuals are incomplete as they are, and compared to others, they do not measure up. In essence, the commodification machine of Western hegemony pumps out the idea that people are not enough: They are too old, too fat, too skinny, not smart enough, not womanly enough or manly enough, and that the solution is to buy products, services, procedures, or some purchased solution to compensate. According to West (1982), hegemonic culture is "a culture successful at persuading people to consent to their oppression and exploitation" (p. 119). When a culture is dominated by a worldview that measures personal success based on economic wealth, it creates a polarization and stratification where there is a class of those who have success and those who do not. As Katz (2006) suggests, "Hegemony refers to a certain way of life and thought being dominant, which is diffused throughout society to inform norms, values and tastes, political practices, and social relations (p. 335).

Some recent studies have suggested that materialism may be associated with dissatisfaction, depression, isolation, anxiety, and anger, not happiness. At the same time some academic researchers are studying ayahuasca as a potential cure to these exact issues. Furthermore, the values of materialism seem to work in opposition to other human needs, such as connection, safety, and authenticity (Eckersley, 2006, p. 13). This is not to suggest that materialism is the only source of such issues, but that materialism is one significant influence, and a thread directly linked to the priorities of Western cultures. A pitfall of Western hegemony is the manner in which nearly every aspect of life is reduced down to a form of commodification. Certainly the fashion, cosmetic, and beauty industries prey on people who feel inadequate. Orbach (1986) explains,

> The images that are presented in advertising are designed to create an illusion, a fantasy ideal that will keep women continually consuming. Advertisers are well aware of the insecurities that most women feel about their own bodies. The influential power of the diet, fashion, cosmetic and beauty industries, and their advertising strategies, target this, and their profits are sustained on the enormity of the body insecurity. (p. 79)

Naomi Wolf (2002) goes even further in talking about the damage caused by these industries noting, "the advertisers who make women's mass culture possible depend on making women feel bad enough about their faces and bodies to spend more money on worthless or pain inducing products than they would if they felt innately beautiful" (p. 84). There certainly appears to be a corresponding set of industries that exploit men as well. Viagra commercials, weight loss industries, beer commercials, and other cultural "ideals" of masculinity leave men feeling incomplete as well. The byproduct of Western hegemony seems to be an increase in escapism, lack of connection to others, lack of meaning, disassociation, and discontent. These all lead to some of the major cultural issues of our time including depression and anxiety, from which advertisers and big pharmaceutical companies profit. In the United States alone, 40 million adults over the age of 18 are affected by anxiety. Anxiety disorders and the treatment of them costs the United States more than $42 billion per year. At the same time, approximately 20 million adults over the age of 18 suffer from depression each year as well (Anxiety and Depression Association of America, 2015). My research data suggest that the ayahuasca experience helps people feel less isolated, and find a deeper sense of meaning and purpose, along with more social support, from attending ayahuasca ceremonies.

ANTIDOTAL MOVEMENT

The antidote to the personal trappings of Western hegemony on a personal level refers to a movement toward self-determination. I am using self-determination not in reference to a country or a state controlling its own destiny, but in the way of individuals becoming free from limitations and barriers to happiness and freedom. The theme of self-determination on both state and individual levels are similar, however. Clements (2004) defines self-determination as, "the ability of people/s to name, create and control their own history" (p. 66). The woundings of Western hegemony on individuals often times prevent them from dreaming a new future, moving through emotional trappings, and being free from trauma and pain. The ayahuasca experience provides opportunities for individuals to find healing on all levels: emotional, physical, mental, and spiritual. This is why the ayahuasca experience can be so profound in its healing potential, helping individuals to heal and transform their lives, which then strengthens connections within the individual's family and community. The First Nations Indigenous peoples such as the Anishinabek think of health and healing as having four components, which correspond to the four directions of the medicine wheel. These areas of health include the physical, mental, spiritual, and emotional (Wilson, 2003, pp. 87-88). These four areas are precisely the same levels being healed within the ayahuasca experience. Healing ceremonies, not only ayahuasca ceremonies, are undertaken to help people move through feelings of hopelessness and despair, and to see their innate power. Cajete (1994) mentions that the highest goal of Indigenous education is to help each individual realize and experience completeness in his or her life (p. 211). Cajete seems to be pointing to the process of coming to completeness that people oftentimes experience after working with ayahuasca.

The process of healing with various methods, ceremonies, and processes can be found within Indigenous cultures' cosmologies worldwide. For example, Atkinson (2002) encouraged a group of Australian Aboriginal peoples to write and tell their personal and collective healing stories in a program called, "Al-li: Fire and Water, Anger and Grief" (p. 93). I appreciate the unique and thorough way one of the participants named "Jackie" describes healing:

> Healing is a really confusing word. When I first thought of it, I thought I would go along and all this pain was going to be healed, but now I know healing means learning. Learning about yourself--learning about looking at things in a different way. Understanding how those things came to be. Owning your things, but not taking on board other people's things. Being responsible for what you are responsible for, but not for other people's responsibilities. Learning how to deal with different situations-how to interact with people-how to lessen conflict-seeing your own things differently. (p. 140)

Conventional medicine has been examining the healing potential of ayahuasca as a remedy for a variety of illnesses and issues, including finding spiritual purpose and spiritual meaning (Kjellgren, Eriksson, & Norlander, 2009), healing from trauma (Mate, 2013; Nielson & Megler, 2014), treating addictions (Brierley & Davidson, 2012; Mabit, 2007; Thomas, Lucas, Capler, Tupper & Martin, 2013), and treating depression (Palladino, 2009; Sobiecki, 2013). Ayahuasca, within an Indigenous framework, has the potential to act as a source of healing for many of the ills that stem from Western hegemony because it works holistically. 4

The following table includes a complete list of the interview partic-

Interview Participant	Gender	Age	First year taking Ayahuasca	Approx. times taking ayahuasca	Interview Form
Participant 1	Male	52	2012	14 times	In person
Participant 2	Female	40	2012	21 times	In person
Participant 3	Female	41	2001	40 times	Skype
Participant 4	Male	37	2008	+100 times	Skype
Participant 5	Male	66	2000	+100 times	Skype
Participant 6	Female	39	1998	+100 times	In person
Participant 7	Male	35	2009	25 times	In person
Participant 8	Female	37	2006	40 times	Skype
Participant 9	Female	28	2010	6 times	In person
Participant 10	Male	46	2006	+100 times	In person
Ceremony Leader	Male	52	2004	+400 times	In person

Total Qualitative Participants: Gender, Age, First Year Working with Ayahuasca, Approximate Number of Times Worked with Ayahuasca, and Interview Format.

ipants, including the ayahuasca ceremony leader. The chart is presented so that the reader can clearly see the differences in responses based on both the number of years participants have worked with ayahuasca, and the number of times they have experienced ayahuasca. These differences can be noted in their interview comments, which are included along with each antidote. As a point of clarification, after each comment a participant number is noted as P1, P2, and so on, which corresponds to participant number in the chart below. When there is a quotation from the ceremony leader it is noted as Ceremony Leader.

Comments About the Data. One-hundred percent of interview participants noted that the ayahuasca experience helped them experience healing on a personal or individual level, including transformation, gaining insights about their life, and helping to change unhealthy belief systems. This movement towards self-determination can be seen in the realizations, epiphanies, and examples of healing and transformation that participants mention. The samples provide examples of healing on multiple levels, change, shedding belief systems, and bringing new awareness and perspective to participants about their lives.

Antidote 1: Samples from the Data
-The medicine reminds me to be a better person and what is important to me (P3).
-It's a plant and a beautiful medicine that heals people, heals bodies, heals interpersonal relationships and societal relationships (P4).
-I was in a mild depressive state and had a lot of anxiety and it helped me (P7).
-Brought up childhood fears and trauma for me to face and deal with (P1).
-It's more of an awareness of an internal filing system where memories that are either painful or joyful get fragmented and then the process works to reorganize them or restructure them (P1)
-It's helped me understand myself, let go of things I needed to let go of—personality, thought patterns, lifestyles (P7).
-It was like therapy, but much deeper (P6).
-Doing the hard work on yourself and examining your own shit, and bringing it forward into the world (P2).
-I have come to peace with certain things about being a woman, things that felt stuck before (P9).
-Self-love from the ayahuasca, which has been a huge part of the process for

me (P8).
-Learned about myself and my traumas in my life, my family heritage, and my ancestral lineage (P8).
-I have changed how I treat self, others, the way I behave, and the person that I am (P9).

Discussion About Antidote 1

Based on the existing literature, I expected the ayahuasca experience to be effective at helping individuals heal, learn, and grow. Ayahuasca has been shown to relieve depression, anxiety, post-traumatic stress disorder (PTSD), and to heal forms of trauma. Ayahuasca has also been shown to help people find a connection to their spirituality and to assist them in having meaning and purpose in their lives. I also assumed that ayahuasca would be effective at helping individuals move away from the destructive influences of Western hegemony on toward self-determination, which my results confirmed.

One of the unique features of the ayahuasca experience is that each individual appears to have a different experience, and participants report that the ayahuasca experience is never the same twice. The ayahuasca experience, therefore, seems to be individualistic in how it helps each person in a somewhat different way and effects change in different ways. Both my qualitative and quantitative research data confirmed that there seems to be a connection between working with ayahuasca and movement away from the personal trappings of Western hegemony. These samples from the qualitative interviews all point to the healing process the ayahuasca experience provides for people. This power of ayahuasca to assist with personal healing and a movement away from Western hegemonic structures can be found in a few samples from the qualitative interviews:

> -When you sit in ceremony and meet Grandmother Ayahuasca, you learn a lot about yourself. You see where you're stuck and where you are already free. You have this amazing opportunity to really dialogue with the plant spirits and dis-engage from your past, and society's influences. (Ceremony Leader)
> -There is always so much personalization to the experiences that I hear when others share about it too. (P1)

Psychotherapeutic traditions. The first antidote, movement from the personal trappings of Western hegemony towards self-determination, can potentially be found in many traditions, healing, and pedagogical models. Psychotherapy, and other Western forms of healing, also helps individuals learn about, and loosen the grip of Western hegemonic institutional forces, such as homophobia, classism, racism, sexism, and other forms of institutional bias. These psychologically based forms of healing sometimes assist individuals in understanding how the covert forces of hegemony work so that individuals can find solutions that lead towards self-determination and freedom from these destructive influences. The ayahuasca experience, situated within the Indigenous worldview, looks at self-determination as something healed through relationality and specifically through ceremony and ritual.

Psychotherapy, however, often only focuses on helping individuals to understand themselves better, and to learn coping skills. The psychotherapy process often ignores the external forces of hegemony or social influences that may affect the individual. Psychotherapy tends to focus only on the individual because it is oriented towards the Western worldview. Western models of healing tend to focus on the individual and the individual's healing process, and not on creating larger community or family-level change as part of the healing process. Brief therapy, for example, focuses on assisting clients in finding solutions to their personal issues and to learn to focus on inner resources and strengths (de Shazer, 1985). These are important skills to develop in the person's healing process, but they are different than the type of personal changes individuals tend to go through by working with ayahuasca. The Western model of healing is in contrast to the Indigenous worldview that looks at healing as done on behalf of the larger world along with the individual level.

Antidote 2:
Movement from Individuality and "Survival of the Fittest" Towards Relationality and a Kinship-Focused Orientation

This antidote and its movement suggest that ayahuasca helps move people from the Western hegemonic structure of individualism and "survival of the fittest" towards "relationality" and kinship-focused. At the heart of the solution to the Western hegemonic notions of individualism and survival of the fittest is the concept of relationality, whereby humans strive to have healthy relationships with other people, with the environment, with the larger cosmos, with ideas, and with one's self (Wilson, 2008). This movement happens when individuals working with ayahuasca change their orientation and values from self-concern toward being concerned with others.

Western Hegemonic Structure

Western hegemony prioritizes the ideas of survival of the fittest and individualism. Conversely, the Indigenous worldview values interdependence and collectivism (Harkness, Super, & Tijen (2000). Puchala (2005) argues, "Hegemony connotes the domination of the weak by the strong, the many by the few. It implies the institutionalization of privilege, consequent inequality in the distributions of various values, and the injustices inherent in inequality" (p. 571). This definition highlights a polarized worldview where some people succeed at the expense of others. This form of hegemony creates social values where there is a zero sum gain, whereby some people succeed while others fail. Okazaki, David, and Abelmann (2008) argue that Western scholarship, which is directly connected to the forces of Western cultural hegemony, tend to frame and represent non-Western cultures as "other." This framing of non-Western cultures as "other" promotes the notion of the West being the standard and being the norm (p. 92). The deep structure of Western hegemony seems to be entrenched in the belief that the aim of life is success and seeking personal gain, which is valued above others' success and happiness. This belief seems to suggest that one only be concerned with one's own small family unit, and not consider the global community of humanity.

Western cultures place a high significance on individuation and its implications of self-perceived freedom to pursue one's goals without concern of the impacts on others. The Jungian model of individuation focuses on an individual's autonomous identity (Jung, 1981). In other words, individuals are associated with themselves and their self-pursuits, beliefs, and individual happiness. Western culture tends to value individual pursuits and individual needs as above the needs of anyone or anything else. Hofstede (2011) concludes that people from individualistic cultures think and conceive of themselves as "I." Members of collective cultures, such as Indigenous peoples, think of themselves as not only family members by identification, but as part of extended families. In other words, people from collectivist cultures, such as most Indigenous people, tend to think of themselves as "we" not as "I" (pp. 8-9). Like other forms of hegemony, individualism and sociocentrism are so entrenched and prevalent within Western culture that, to most people, they seem normal and insignificant. Yet, this form of Western hegemony is destructive and creates polarization within families, groups, communities, and ultimately a polarized world.

Antidotal Movement

My research data suggest that one potential antidote to the hegemonic force of individualism is connected to moving towards Indigenous relational models, whereby people, places, and things are viewed as relatives. Deloria and Wildcat (2001) explain that within an Indigenous model, the "highest good" implies that humans value relationships and interdependencies, and act from a moral viewpoint when interacting with others (p. 96). Relationality as a cultural model means that life is viewed through the lens of how people, places, and things are all related (Cajete, 1994; Deloria & Wildcat, 2001; Simpson, 2000; Wilson, 2008). Relationality also refers to the relationships between things, including the relationships between the natural and unnatural world, and relationships between and among people. An example of the concept of Indigenous relationality is the use of the Cree word nisitohtamowin that means understanding, but understanding one's self in relation to others (Kovach, 2009, p. 58).

Most Indigenous models of the role individuals play within the larger community put forth the idea that relationships (familial, communal, cosmological) are the focus and the priority, because we exist in an interdependent web of life. As a result, being an active community member, having good relationships within one's family, within one's community, and with one's environment are integrated into cultural values, and therefore become priorities. This is a sharp contrast to more Western ideas of self-fulfillment viewed as a priority with minimal concern for others. According to East African Indigenous scholar Semali (1999a), "Indigenous knowledge does not derive its origins or meaning from the individual, but from the collective epistemological understanding and rationalization of the community" (p. 309). This collective epistemological understanding also includes recognizing elders and elder wisdom as important in the learning process, along with the importance of having respect for multi-generations within a community context. Western hegemony, which tends to promote youth as the goal and encourages industries to try to sell people on looking youthful, creates polarization within families and communities whereby there are few meaningful opportunities for multi-generations to connect and dialogue. Cajete (2000) asserts that through community, native people learn their personhood and identity. Community is also the place individuals come to understand relationship, responsibility, and community participation (pp. 85-87). The confusion of autonomy with independence encourages a perception by individuals that they are separate from others and the environment in which they live, and so from the very things that affect their lives (Eckersley, 2006, p. 13). The Western notion of individualism, meaning people are separate and not innately interconnected, drives feelings and perceptions of loneliness, separation, and isolation.

Various types of ceremonies, rituals, and initiations happen frequently within Indigenous cultures. These ceremonies and rituals are based on communal knowledge transfer, and experiential learning, and are situated within a different worldview than Western cultural paradigms (Cajete, 1994; Deloria & Wildcat, 2001. Ayahuasca done within a ceremonial context is able to work as a meaningful ritual and ceremony, and fulfill an initiatory purpose, and is grounded within an experiential learning format. Community ceremonies within some Australian Aboriginal cultures are done to help with illness, to connect with the cycles of nature, to help return creative energy to those feeling helpless or distressed, and assist in healing conflicts (Atkinson, 2002, p. 33). Ayahuasca ceremonies also provide the opportunity to help heal illness and reconnect to creative energy. Public ceremonies and private rituals give families and communities shared experiences of healing and transformation. In turn, these experiences become integrated into the language of family and community relations (Castellano, 2004, p. 101). Ceremonies as structures for collective meaning and healing are common among Indigenous peoples, and are vehicles to help remedy isolation, depression, and conflict. These Indigenous examples of the power of ritual and ceremony to effect change an individual, family, and community levels all point to the power of the ayahuasca experience as a way to combat hegemony.

Comments About the Data. One-hundred percent of the qualitative interview participants commented that the ayahuasca experience shifted how they viewed and related to their families, communities, and friends; that they developed more compassion and empathy for those around them. The samples from the data demonstrate a movement to relationality and kinship-focused. This theme can be seen clearly in the sample comments and how people shift from being only concerned with their own welfare and happiness towards being concerned about others.

ANTIDOTE 2: SAMPLES FROM THE DATA
-Everyone is coming to ceremony and has their own set of concerns, problems, issues or past, hurt and wounds, and once you see that, you realize we are all in this together (P7).
-It has taught me a great reverence for other people in general).
-Over time you see yourself in others. You begin to go to ceremony not only for yourself and to help with your own healing, but to help others and focus on their healing and well being as well (Ceremony Leader).
-I have a deeper relationship with what it means to pray in community (P8).
-More aware of what others are going through (P4).
-Greater sense of responsibility for the world (P3).
-Supporting people in my spiritual community is now a priority (P2).
-The medicine put me more in tune with how people work, see deeper into people (P4).
-Feeling other's suffering (P3).
-To hold myself to a higher standard and do right by people (P2).
-Be more compassionate and less judgmental (P10).
-I have the desire to give back to others (P9).
-Caring for others and giving what you can is more important and more rewarding (P2)
-Seeing greater beauty in people (P4).

ANTIDOTE 2: ANTIDOTAL MOVEMENT FOUND IN THE QUANTITATIVE DATA
On the question of acting with compassion and empathy, these statements were posed:

Before taking ayahuasca, acting with compassion and empathy was important to me.
After taking ayahuasca, acting with compassion and empathy is more important to me.

This question set looks at empathy and compassion and points to the notion of relationality, whereby extending care to people outside one's self is important to individuals. Looking at compassion and empathy seem to be ways to examine a potential movement from individuality and a survival-of-the-fittest mentality toward kinship focus. In both groups (the group who has worked with ayahuasca more than 50 times and the group who has worked with ayahuasca less than 50 times), there is a movement, after working with ayahuasca, towards acting with compassion and empathy as more important. In the group of people who have worked with ayahuasca more than 50 times, 100% of participants agree or strongly agree that after working with ayahuasca, acting with compassion and empathy is more important to them. In the group who have worked with ayahuasca less than 50 times, 94% agree or strongly agree that after working with ayahuasca acting with compassion is more important to them.

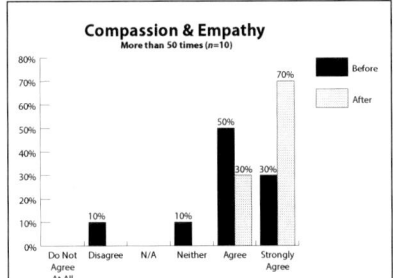 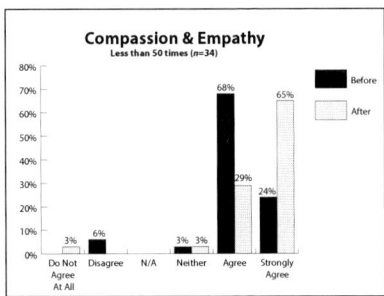

Comparison of acting with compassion and empathy: More than 50x ayahuasca versus less than 50x ayahuasca.

On the question of putting one's own needs above those of others, two statements were posed:

Before ayahuasca, I put my needs and desires above others including my friends, family, and community.

After ayahuasca, I am less focused on my own needs and desires and more concerned with the needs of others including my family, friends, and community.

Given that ayahuasca has the potential to change people's life priorities, I would expect a large number of participants to disagree that they put their own needs above others. As a result, it makes sense that a large number disagreed to the statement, "Before ayahuasca, I put my needs and desires above others including my friends, family, and community." In the group of participants who have worked with ayahuasca more than 50 times, 80% agree or strongly agree that after working with ayahuasca, they are less focused on their needs and desires and more concerned with the needs of others. However, in the group of participants who have worked with ayahuasca less than 50 times, 53% agree or strongly agree that they are less focused on their needs and desires and more concerned with the needs of others. This difference in the two groups of people who work with ayahuasca (those who have worked with it more than 50 times and those who have worked with it less) seems to suggest that possibly, over time, people who work with ayahuasca become less focused on their own needs and more concerned with the needs of others. The short qualitative interviews also showed that people tend to move towards thinking and helping others. This movement aligns with Antidote 2's movement from individualism towards relationality.

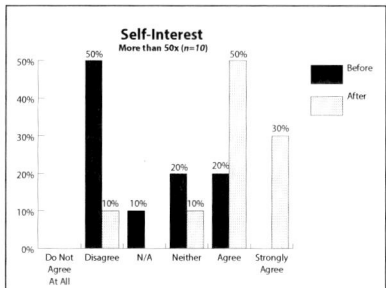 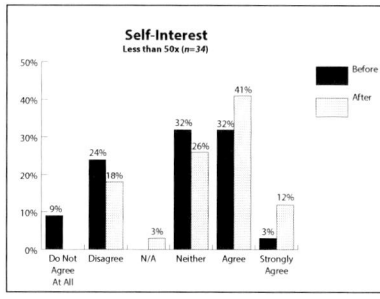

Comparison of self/other needs: More than 50x ayahuasca versus less than 50x ayahuasca.

On the question of one's thinking of the long-term consequences of his or her actions, two statements were posed:

Before taking ayahuasca, I thought about the long-term effects and consequences of my actions.
After taking ayahuasca, I think about the long-term effects and consequences of my actions.

I am putting this question under the category of relationality, because it points to some of the basic premises of relational values, specifically, how one's actions affect others, including humans and nonhumans. With both sets of research participants, there is nearly a shift towards agreeing and strongly agreeing to thinking about long-term consequences of one's actions after working with ayahuasca. The group of participants who have experienced ayahuasca more than 50 times moved from 50% of participants agreeing or strongly agreeing that they thought about the long-term effects and consequences of their actions before working with ayahuasca to 80% agreeing or strongly agreeing after working with ayahuasca. In the participants who have worked with ayahuasca less than 50 times, 65% of participants agreed or strongly agreed that they thought about the long-term consequences of their actions before working with ayahuasca, 85% of participants who worked with ayahuasca more than 50 times agreed or strongly agreed than they thought about the long-term consequences of their actions, a difference of 10%. This increase in long-term thinking seems significant to a potential movement away from individuality towards relationality.

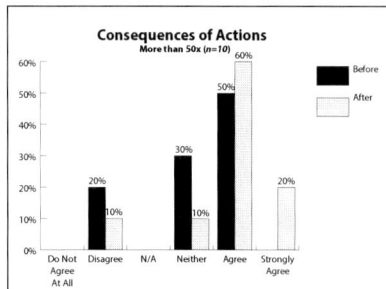 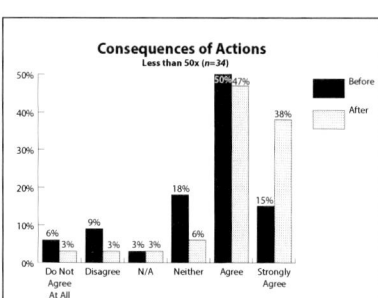

Comparision of long-term consequences of actions: More than 50x ayahuasca versus less than 50x ayahuasca.

Discussion about Antidote 2

Another way to examine relationality is to look at whether or not the ayahuasca experience results in an increase in compassion and empathy for others. My quantitative data showed that in the group of people who have worked with ayahuasca more than 50 times, 100% of participants agree or strongly agree that after working with ayahuasca, acting with compassion and empathy is more important to them. De Rios and Rumrrill (2008) suggest that ayahuasca can enhance empathy and can bring about social harmony by allowing people to understand each other more thoroughly. They argue that ayahuasca also sharpens social awareness, resulting in social bonding (p. 6). The social bonding and social healing De Rios and Rumrrill (2008) mention points to the antidotal movement from individuality towards relationality. One participant from the short qualitative interviews highlighted the ability of ayahuasca to work on multiple relational levels at once, which supports the assertion that ayahuasca can bring about social bonding, saying, "It is a plant and a beautiful medicine that heals people, heals bodies, heals interpersonal relationships, and societal relationships." Healing interpersonal relationships along with societal relationships is situated within the definitions of relationality. The comments from an anonymous respondent highlight a related theme in the qualitative data, which shows the ayahuasca experience might bring about a change in how individuals value others outside themselves. The following comment from this respondent offers specific clues on how the ayahuasca experience works in an organic way to open people up:

> While I've always had a strong desire for community connection, support, and intention to improve it, I think the medicine and ceremony have helped me internalize the experience that love and compassion are the foundation for these connections and that without love and compassion, I can participate and play a part in improving my community, but the true connection occurs through love and compassion and subsequently non-judgment. I think ayahuasca and the ayahuasca community has helped me feel and express compassion and empathy in a more natural, authentic way.

The comments from both interview and questionnaire participants suggest a distinct movement towards relationality inspired by the ayahuasca experience. At the same time, both sets of comments also show a movement towards the Indigenous worldview, and away from the Western worldview. Within the Indigenous worldview, community participation and the value of community is viewed as highly important and one of the top values. Within the literature about ayahuasca, very little is discussed regarding helping individuals shift their orientation from individualistic towards more kinship-focused, however. In my observation, the theme of ayahuasca potentially working to help individuals become more relational in their orientation does not often surface in the literature about ayahuasca, especially in Indigenous cultures, because most ayahuasca leaders and ayahuasca cultures are collectivist in nature. In addition, it appears that Westerners who lead ayahuasca ceremonies, along with those who regularly participate in ayahuasca ceremonies, may already be oriented towards an Indigenous worldview versus a Western worldview.

Stages of Maturity: Erikson and Kegan. There are many ways people can move from individuality towards relationalty, however. This movement may happen naturally during the stages of healthy maturity. Developmental psychologist Erik Erikson's (1963) model of early social and moral development present eight distinct stages that address each stage of a person's lifetime. Within each stage of development, there is a psychosocial crisis along with a corresponding virtue associated with the stage. Within Erikson's model, the psychosocial crisis associated with adulthood is "generativity versus stagnation." The virtue associated with adulthood is "care." Part of the adulthood stage of development, according to Erikson, is learning to develop a sense of caring, concern, and empathy for others. This increased focus on care and concern corresponds, in some ways, to the movement towards relationality found within the ayahuasca-based antidotes to Western hegemony.

Dombeck (2007) offers another layer in understanding how people can move through the stages of social maturity. In Dombeck's description, he drew inspiration from Robert Kegan's work, Evolving Self (1992), which said:

> New layers of social/emotional development occur as people become able to finally see themselves in increasingly larger and wider social perspective. For example, the moment I am able to understand for the first time what another person is thinking or feeling, I have made a sort of leap forwards out of subjectivity (me being trapped in my own perspective) and into a view of the world that is a little more objective. If I can understand what someone else is thinking and feeling, I can also imagine myself as I must look through their eyes and my self-understanding becomes that much more objective. This sort of expanded awareness represents an emergence from

embeddedness in my own subjective perspective and the growth of my ability to see things from multiple perspectives at once.

These stages of maturity described by both Erikson and Dombeck may describe the organic process which individuals go through as they re-examine their lives and their priorities. As a natural part of the aging process, they may naturally gravitate towards what is most important to them on a more essential level, and move away from the less meaningful trappings of individuality. This shift in values may follow a natural sequence as put forth by Erikson, whereby caring for others becomes a higher priority. At the same time, Dombeck's comments about expanding one's awareness to see more complexity and view multiple perspectives may also shift simply as a byproduct of becoming a more mature person and having more life experience. These stages of maturity shown in the models of Erikson and Dombeck do not include a critique of the covert hegemonic forces that are steeped in the beliefs of individualism and in survival of the fittest as key covert paradigms that are supported and adopted in the undercurrent of Western culture. Nor do Erikson and Dombeck explore gender differences in development. Carol Gilligan (1982), for example, explains that women tend to understand themselves in relationship to others and through their relationships, while men tend to understand themselves through individuating from others. These biases in Erikson and Dombeck's work point to possible influences of Western hegemonic thinking.

The ayahuasca experience, on the other hand, is not based on a linear pattern of chronological stages of development. Instead, ayahuasca tends to propel people towards adopting various elements of the Indigenous worldview and rearranging their lives and priorities in the process. These shifts that occur during the maturing process are different than the antidotal movement towards relationality I am describing, which is rooted in Indigenous wisdom and an Indigenous worldview. Relationality within an Indigenous worldview means that life is viewed through the lens of how people, places, and things are all related (Cajete, 1994; Deloria & Wildcat, 2001; Wilson, 2008). Relationality implies a shift towards interdependence and extending empathy and caring beyond one's immediate family or friends.

Nor do these developmental models address the glaring issue that Western hegemony, which supports a number of "isms," seems to purposefully create community stratification and moves away from relationality. By "stratification," I am referring to a Western model whereby mixed generations rarely interact; whereby class stratification creates social polarization based on the haves and the have-nots; whereby Whites and minorities are not necessarily encouraged to interact; whereby men and women are supposedly in a gender war; whereby gay and straight people are viewed in opposition to each other; whereby Republicans and Democrats are seen as complete opposites in their beliefs and only vote along party lines, rather than engaging with issues; whereby those who identify with Judeo-Christian backgrounds depict people of other faiths as unusual or alternative, and so on. In all of these cases, the forces of Western hegemony create and support the notion of "other," and when a group is labeled "other" they are then dehumanized, objectified, and depersonalized in the process of being treated poorly. We currently see this in the dramatic rise in Islamaphobia, whereby the cultural narrative along with the media narratives depict followers of Islam as terrorists and dangers to society, which has resulted in a spike in hate crimes and hate speech. These forces of polarization are in contrast to relationality and the Indigenous worldview that attempts to bring communities together, not pull them apart.

Anitdote 2: Interview with Sobonfu Some (10/13/2015) on the Dagara Tradition of Relationality and Community

It was a great honor to be able to interview Sobonfu Some. Sobonfu, whose name means "keeper of the rituals" travels the world on a healing mission, sharing the rich spiritual life and culture of her native land Burkina Faso, which ranks as one of the world's poorest countries. Recognized by the village elders as possessing special gifts from birth, Sobonfu's destiny was foretold before her birth, as is the custom of the Dagara Tribe of Burkina Faso, and was fostered by early education in ritual and initiation in preparation for her life's work. Dagara rituals involve healing and preparing the mind, body, spirit and soul to receive the spirituality that is all around us. "It is always challenging to bring the spiritual into the material world, but it is one of the only ways we can put people back in touch with the earth and their inner values." Since the beginning of her journey in the West, Sobonfu has traveled extensively throughout North America and Europe, conducting workshops on spirituality, ritual, the sacred, and intimacy. Her work has moved African spiritual practices from the realm of anthropology to a place alongside the world's great spiritual tradition, with a message of profound significance and practical application in the lives of Westerners. While she does not work with, nor necessarily encourages work with ayahuasca, her teachings about the role of community and some of the challenges facing Western people are profound and touch on some of the same points I have explored in my research.

One of the problems I want to talk to you about is the Western notion of individualism and people feeling stuck, and not connected to others.

Sobonfu Some: It is a challenge that we are all facing. Even places in Africa, where the community existed, I am finding out that things are falling apart — as modernization creeps in. The way the government sells it to them is that this is good for you. And then they wake up the next day and they don't have the land and they don't have their ancestral worshipping place anymore; they are just homeless as though they never had a home. So it has become a global problem.

But people, especially in the city, have been so pulled into believing that their problems lie in the fact that they are not modern enough and that they don't have a way to make it big in the world, by Western standards, and that is why they are having problems. So when you talk to them about the rich culture they have that can be used as a problem-solving tool, they look at you like "huh?"

The last time I was in Burkina (Burkina Faso is a small country in West Africa), I met with some students who just had a visiting teacher from Japan who basically told them that Burkina needs to look into its own culture to find the solutions to their problems. The students responded, "But, like, where?" People don't even see that there is value in what they have.

There seems to be a difference in a worldview that values collectivism or community-oriented values, which then inspire a different set of actions than those from individualistic cultures who have an individualistic worldview.

SS: There is a big difference when you have been brought up in a community setting where your belief system has been supported by that community versus being born in a nuclear family in a place where community does not have such a strong pull on the individual. There are bits and pieces that definitely make your connection to other people more difficult because you don't see how this person who may be crawling on the ground could be of value and of use to you tomorrow or today, even. So, in my own upbringing, being brought up in that system where everything is connected, and nothing you come across is just a random accident. In fact, in the Dagara tradition there is no word for "accident." If you hear it the word "accident" being used, it is from the French word, because (Burkina) is a French colony.

In an article I wrote for a collection of essays called Belonging, I was trying to say that I feel that my identity is tied to so many things. It is tied to the land. It is tied to the trees that surround the land. It is tied to my ancestors. It is tied to the people who are around. It is tied to the animals that I grew up knowing and them knowing me. To try to identify myself as a separate person outside of those things and their values, you don't really get a full picture of me. So, when I am talking about the baobab tree, for someone who has never seen a baobab tree and its impact and influence on my life, they don't know what I'm talking about. Yet, that baobab tree is part of what makes me who I am. It is part of my DNA.

So values are attached to things that can serve you into some profit.

But it helps you to know why you are who you are, and why you behave and think the way you do. So, having been brought up in that context, the simple fact, for instance, that when I grew up I never slept by myself my entire life. Then I ended up in Michigan, and all of a sudden, it was just another person and me and I had to spend the night by myself. I went crazy. I thought something was wrong. Fears that I didn't have before, I started to have those fears. Reactions that I didn't have before, I started to have those too. Coming from that community to this isolated place, I started to experience things. In French, they call it the "cockroach." It is a process where you slowly realize, and it slowly gets to you, that you are separate, and you are out there and no one has your back. And nothing in your world begins to make sense. You basically go crazy, but you don't know that you're going crazy.

When I would write letters back home and I would explain what I was going through here (in the United States), people would go, "Why is she thinking that? Why can't she go to the elders over there? Don't you have peers you can share what is going on with you?" And I'm going, "People, I don't speak English," that's one. So, I have a huge barrier. Number two, I basically don't have neighbors that I can go to who would even open the door for me. It was difficult for them to understand that if you don't know someone, that the person won't take you in, even if you are in trouble. I was facing a huge cultural difference that I did not even know how to bridge.

I think you are really describing how we are raised in the West, at least most of what you are talking about reflects how I was raised. I was not taught or grew up feeling connected to nature, the larger community, or to those around me.

SS: That is how I experienced it; by feeling sick. Then I realized, there is something not right here. My body started to not even take the food in. I had to go through a process at home to learn how to realign myself, my spirit and my soul with the spirit of the land and accept what is being offered by it. I didn't even know my system was at war with what I was encountering.

Do you think that is because in the West people are not in relationship with the elders, nature and with our neighbors, and again wholly adopted an individualistic worldview?

SS: I don't really think that it all just came like that. When you go to other parts of the West, in Europe for example, you see that the connection is still there. There is still a value that is attached to the land that is beyond its monetary value. The ways that people interact with one another is not entirely individualistic.

The second thing is that when the Industrial Revolution started, in order to sell the idea of a job to people, they had to come with all kinds of things (to buy). First, they created the jobs and told people to go to work, and then you can get money. People went to work and got the money, but now what do you do with it. So, they realized that people didn't know what to do with their money. Then, they started to introduce the company store. The company store started to get you into debt. Then, you had to basically owe the rest of your life to the company store. In those times, the company store still looked after your interests. So, you didn't feel that you were going to get dropped. That was not sufficient. We still rebelled. Some people still kept doing their farming, their art work, and still had the same results, even better because they were not indebted. So, then they had to create retirement to entice us. So, then retirement came as the idea that basically makes it worth it to stop living your purpose, so you can give yourself to this entity. And, when you retire, then you can go do the thing you actually love, the thing you came here with. So, even though you feel the inner struggle, you think, "At least I have a roof over my head and retirement to look forward to." And, when we retire, we have all these plans that you have created for yourself.

Some of us got excited and got rid of a system that was not really taking are of our needs, and excited ourselves into the other world. So, what has been the challenge for people, who are artists, is that they realize the system is really not working for them. They kind of are the voice for the rest of us because they don't fit the mold and they refuse to fit the mold. And that is why, by government standards, artists are kind of useless, because they don't really contribute the way they want them to contribute. It is because they haven't figured out a way to take that passion for your purpose away. If they knew how to do that, they would convince the artists also. But it would be a great mistake, because artists, in a way, keep the thing of the unspoken in the psyche alive, in the heart and soul of the people. So that, even though we may be going crazy, you look at the creation of an artist, and it takes you back to that sacred place, and you are okay again.

In the village you are from in Africa, is the economic system based on this allure of retirement and making money as opposed to expressing one's gifts or barter?

SS: In the cities, yes. In the villages no, it is still based on your gifts, what you were born with.

That was my impression, but I didn't want to be naïve about it. I thought there was still some integrity of it functioning in a good way, which is rare and seems almost impossible in the West.

SS: It is difficult and the government is not making it easy for people either. About five years ago, people still bartered in my village, it was the main way they traded. More and more, there is pressure from the government to make that money. The seed that is planted in the young people is that your elders are really backwards. They are old-fashioned, and they don't really understand today's world. So, if you follow us, we will get you into the new. A lot of people go into that, and, by the time they realize it, they are already deep in it. Then, they don't know how to get out of it because now there is a hook in them from the government, and now they see what they have lost in terms of their soul, and in terms of their own values that they grew up with.

How does that tie into the grief rituals you do? Can you compare the rituals where you grew up versus how they are conducted in the West? Because you have been doing this for a long time and seen a lot of people in the West.

SS: I have been doing grief rituals in the West for a couple of decades at least. My whole life, starting when I was in my mom's womb, I have been participating in them. The grief ritual in the villages is a human need that has to be expressed—if the people are going to be healthy, if the people are going to keep an alignment with their purpose, and so on. There are certain frictions in life that bring certain kinds of tainting to the soul that need to be cleansed. Just like if you always wore the same shirt, every once in a while, it needs to be cleansed. If not, you yourself wouldn't want to wear it because it smelled so bad. The same way, our soul needs some kind of purging so that it can be reborn, so it can recreate itself. Those rituals have been happening for thousands of years in my tribe. I don't even know when it started.

The grief ritual does not have a mono-focal purpose. It really deals with all the losses that an individual can ever experience in their lives. From a loss of vision, a loss of purpose, a loss of a job, a loss of a loved one, the losses with all the crisis that are going on all over the world, etc. Because of its openness and welcoming of all the different issues, it addresses the crisises of the human soul. You realize you had something precious and you then you wake up the next day and you no longer have it. So your soul needs to grieve the fact that that thing is now missing. Not so you can replace it with something else, but that you can remember how much that thing was important to you. It leaves the space there to heal, because if you don't, our human tendency is to replace it with junk. Then, two days later, we go and repeat the old pattern. So, in the village, the way the grief ritual happens is that it happens out in the open. It can be because someone has died, or because someone is going through a personal initiation, and so on. All reasons for having the ritual are valid. In the village, you have people who are gatekeepers, making sure they are channeling the energy to the right spot. So, in that sense, you can grieve anywhere if the energy is channeled to the grief alter.

The difference between the grief ritual in the village and the one we do here (in the United States) is, first of all, you do not always have a space to grieve. So, sometimes the grieving happens behind closed doors, or sometimes, when I have done it in jail—they are not going to release prisoners to you to take out in the wide open. Sometimes, we do the grief ritual in places that are very challenging to work with, but necessary. The grief ritual is flexible enough so that it can be worked to fit those environments. In the West, people need to have their meal times. So you stop, you eat, and stop for the night. In the village, if you see them stopping it is because one of the musical instruments needs tuning or has broken, a musician needs to stop, or there is something about the ritual that needs to be discussed that they have stopped to discuss. It goes on from the day into the night. When you are tired, you go rest. When you are hungry, you go find food and you eat. In fact, it is common to see mom and dad are crying because grandmother died, and their child is there crying because they are hungry. It is all part of the grieving; no grief is out of place. It is open to anyone, including strangers. Some rituals may not necessarily be that open, but the grief ritual is very open. You can drive through the village and see they are doing the grief ritual, you stop and do your own grieving, and you keep going. No one ever asks you why you are there. Everyone understands that if you stopped, something in you needs honoring, and that is why you stopped. Those are some of the big differences.

Isn't frequency an issue too? It would seem that if they are happening often in the village versus in the West, where someone may only attend one of your events, it might not be as curative. It seems similar to ayahuasca in that way, that people might work with ayahuasca frequently enough to discharge negative or stored pain. It becomes how one lives one's life, as opposed to an occasional experience that is not contextualized in one's life every once in a while.

SS: Absolutely. The making of the ritual is the same, but the making of the people depends on what happens in the ritual. You can create the ritual the same, but because the land you are on is different, the people who come are different, you end up with a completely different result. I have heard people over the years come to me and say, "This one was different from the other." Yes, because it needs to be, because we are not on the same piece of land, and the people who have shown up are not the same. Even doing the grief ritual in California, and then doing it in the Midwest is different. I do it in England and it is different, and it is different when I do it in Germany. So you start to see that there are influences from the land itself and from the spirits themselves, and from the people—and these things influence the ritual, which we often do not think about.

How have you been able to work with someone from an individualistic culture like the United States, whose people tend to have such a different worldview than yours? Specifically, the themes you mentioned in the start, being related to the land, being related to their neighbors, and related to their larger communities, instead of being focused on themselves and their small nuclear families? I guess that is the big question of healing, how to have themselves and everyone else heal at once.

SS: It is not always easy. Some people see they are in trouble and see that they need help, so they are more willing. Other people have to fight themselves tooth and nail because they don't see why it is important to embrace a community. With others, the reluctance comes from the fact that yes, they have been part of some communities, and they have either been let down, or they have been severely abused by that community. So, when you are talking about community, they are sharpening their knives and are ready to take you down, because they are not going to have anything to do with that, even though the program specifically says, we are going to do things in community. So, you end up with different dynamics and different expectations, and you have to work with people to get the to a place where they see that they themselves are the people who they are fighting; you are fighting yourself and you are fighting the damages you have come with. When you are able to see that, then people are willing.

People have to be taught how to be in community. Sometimes, you see someone standing and crying and people are standing there watching, as if it is some kind of phenomenon. People need to be taught, "Hey, this person is crying, it is because something is not going well. It is not necessarily about that person's life." The person may simply be a messenger of something that is happening right there for the whole community that we need to pay attention to. Kind of like children, they don't start to cry because they know someone is going to run to them and tickle them and soothe them. Sometimes they cry because something is not right in the environment they are in. Or, the people around have so much tension, and nobody is addressing it, so the child basically has to let it out for all of us. So people have to be taught to be more caring about each other and give each other permission to show up. In community, showing up is everything. It is not necessarily because you have the answer to everything, but being able to show up for someone who is even ill is critical. Sometimes we are ill because we are lonely.

I can relate. As someone trying to learn to live in community, it can really be a challenge—even a challenge to notions of personal space and my own private time. It becomes quite different than how I was raised where everyone is doing their own thing. I think what you are suggesting is a lot of learning for Western people.

SS: I am laughing, not at you, but I am laughing because I know what is exactly bugging you in that process. It is not because you actually do not want the people to come, it is just that people come with expectations. Sometimes they don't even know that they have expectations. People have been groomed to be entertained. When people show up, they expect you to entertain them. If they are having problems, they expect you to fix their problems. It is not the same as someone showing up in the village and they see that you are working on something, such as yard work; the person is not just going to sit there. They are going to join you because when you are finished with what you are doing, you have time for them. They don't show up and expect you to drop everything and say, "Alright, master, what can I do for you?" However, that is exactly what people expect here. They don't know that they are not showing up in the right way, or they are not dropping-in the right way. They are dropping-in because they want to run away from their life. So, it becomes problematic for the person creating community. If you are coming over and see my farming, help me farm, then I can help you as well. But, you cannot expect me to drop what I am doing, and I tend to you, then you leave, and I still have to go back and do what I have to from scratch.

That also points to the fact that there seems to be so few opportunities for people to come and connect to other people because of so much isolation and most people really don't know what it is like to be in community.

SS: People need to be taught, because if they are not taught, they won't know.

Early on, when you talked about how you define yourself is your relationship with the ancestors and with the trees, for me that is so far from how I was raised. I can imagine these things, but it seems like an abstraction, or a leap of faith, and not a direct experience.

SS: That is just how everybody related. Yes, that is how everyone just related to nature and everything else. That tree is not just a piece of wood or a source of food you just go to. The tree is considered a living being that we need to honor, just like you and I. So, before you take something off a tree, you have to ask permission and you have to explain to the tree why you need this thing. So, the tree is like someone with a home that you go and knock at the door, and they say, "Come in," and you go in, and when you leave, you say, "Goodbye" and "Thank you."

Antidote 3: Movement from Anthropocentrism Towards Viewing the Natural World as Sentient

This antidote shows how the ayahuasca experience influences people to move from the belief that only human beings have consciousness and are the only species of importance towards the view that plants, animals, and the natural world are likewise sentient. For instance, many of the qualitative interview participants reported having reverence for ayahuasca as a living entity, and referring to her as "Grandmother" and as a plant teacher. Furthermore, nearly 100% of the participants in the qualitative and quantitative research components showed a large movement towards viewing the natural world as sentient, therefore moving towards an anthropomorphic view of the natural world.

Western Hegemonic Structure

Western hegemony seems to focus tirelessly on exploitation of resources at any cost, without concern about environmental degradation or sustainability. The Western model of environmental ethics (or lack of ethics) places human beings at the center of the universe, promoting an anthropocentric view of the world. The Indigenous model of environmental ethics positions human beings in relationship with plants, animals, and the natural world. The Western hegemonic model focuses on individual liberty and human-scale utilitarianism, whereas the Indigenous model promotes respect and ecosystem sustainability (Deloria & Wildcat, 2001, p. 96). The Western hegemonic view and treatment of the natural world is based on exploitation, destruction, and disrespect of the earth.

The following examples of environmental degradation clearly demonstrate a distinctly Western belief that nature is subordinate to human beings. The environmental commons is being undermined and threatened by the drive of the market forces to expand corporate ownership of natural resources and increase profits. The drive to exploit resources has paved the way for pollution of the environmental commons. Toxic chemicals in the ground water supply have made water in many places undrinkable and toxic. Water that was previously safe to drink is no longer safe (Ebenstein, 2012). Toxic waste is being shipped all over the world, often to Third World nations, by waste-trading firms (Alston & Brown, 1993, p. 185). Western countries have not significantly decreased their greenhouse gas emissions, in spite of worsening global warming (Church, 2014). Water, which was previously available for free, is rapidly becoming a scarce commodity, and is now often purchased (Bowers, 2005). Acid rain from coal-burning power plants is creating health problems in humans, harming forests and their inhabitants, along with damaging lakes, streams, and other bodies of water. Companies like Monsanto are genetically modifying our food sources without any concern for the impact on the health of human beings, animals, or the environmental costs (Jowitt, 2010). Deforestation is happening at alarming rates, driven by multi-national corporations using the wood and clearcutting for profit. Ecological destruction and warfare are connected, and the United States spends more than any other country on its military and military actions. Warfare, with its often-implied ideological basis, is also destructive to ecosystems and other natural environments (Alston & Brown, 1993, p. 180). These examples of environmental destruction reflect the notion put forth by John Locke that nature has no intrinsic value, aside from serving human beings (Deloria & Wildcat, 2001, p. 75). At the same time, hegemons continue to profit without any concern about environmental destruction or degradation, and the West is told that all of these hegemonic institutions are functioning to improve "progress."

A pointed example of the Western belief that human beings have a right to exploit the natural world for personal gain is the way "bioprospectors" and other researchers exploit and expropriate Indigenous lands and peoples to research, and then steal, traditional herbs and remedies. They oftentimes do so without any concern for environmental destruction or environmental restoration (Four Arrows, 2006; Smith, 1999). For instance, in 1984 an American scientist named Loren Miller applied for a United States patent for a strain of ayahuasca he called "Da Vine" (Miller, 1984; Tupper, 2009). The United States Patent and Trademark Office (USPTO) issued the patent to Miller in 1986 (Tupper, 2009, p. 9). Miller's justification for the patent on Da Vine was that the specific strain of ayahuasca represented a unique strain of the vine due to the color of its petals (Fecteau, 2001, pp. 84-85). In 1999, the Coordinating Body of Indigenous Organizations of the Amazon Basin (CBIOAB) discovered Miller had patented ayahuasca. In response, a group of Indigenous peoples sought legal council to fight the patent (Fecteau, 2001, p. 69). The group received assistance from the Centre for International Environmental Law (CIEL). In 1999, the CBIOAB and the Coalition for Amazonian Peoples and Their Environment filed an appeal to rescind the patent (Tupper, 2009a, p. 9). In 1999, the USPTO revoked the patent. While the patent was revoked, the USPTO rescinded the patent because the plant had been found in the Chicago Field Museum, but it did not address issues about the plant being used for centuries by Indigenous peoples for ceremonial reasons (Fecteau, 2001, p. 86).

Western hegemony, specifically free trade and the Western value of a free marketplace, forces commodification and economics above responsible environmentalism (Humphreys, 1996, p. 223). In the process, the free market ignores the actual costs to the environment and those communities affected by environmental destruction. In the process of exploitation, humans move away from their innate relationship to the natural world, towards a model of domination and separating themselves from nature. Jacobs (1998) explains that Western dominant culture has justified the separation between humans and nature by framing nature and the natural world as dangerous and to be feared (p. 213). Fear is a powerful emotion that hegemons use to create stratification, division, paranoia, and keep individualism, survival of the fittest, and justify an anthropocentric view of the natural world.

ANTIDOTAL MOVEMENT

The antidote to the hegemonic influence of anthropocentrism is to move towards cultivating an anthropomorphic view of nature. In other words, the antidotal movement is to subscribe to Indigenous views of the earth whereby plants, animals, and the natural world are viewed as sentient beings and therefore should be protected and respected. In 2011, for example, Bolivia enacted the "Law of Mother Earth," which granted rights to the earth as equal to humans, much like the corporate structure in the United States offers rights similar rights to corporations as it does to citizens. Passing this law is one example of how to challenge Western hegemonic views of the earth.

An Iroquois belief about personhood integrates Indigenous ideas about relationships between people and their environment to include plants, animals, and other humans. As a result, when the Iroquois conceived of "community," they included humans, as well as plants, animals, and the natural surroundings as "community members" (Deloria & Wildcat, 2001, p. 93). John Mohawk (in Barreiro, 2010) summarizes many ideas found within Indigenous philosophy about the human relationship with the natural world:

> Everybody should be able to give greeting to the Mother Earth...it's a way of us having a relationship with that... It's fundamental: right after people, Earth. Then it goes to grasses, waters, trees, plants, winds, the moon, the stars, the sun, the universe, the whole thing. (p. 275)

Basso (1996) offers additional ways of moving towards an anthropromorphic view of nature through our language patterns and how we name our relationships with the natural world. Basso (1996) asserts that Indigenous peoples' relationship to place and land informs not only their language patterns, but at the same time, their culture and cosmological understanding. Some of the implications of Basso's work are that language patterns and how we name things are demonstrations of our beliefs. For instance, in American Indian sweat lodges, the stones that heat the lodge are referred to as "Grandfathers." It's implied that there is wisdom and respect in these ancient stones, whereas, in Western culture, they are not given that respect. The same respect and love for the natural world can be found in the way many ayahuasca users refer to ayahuasca as "Grandmother." The implication of referring to ayahuasca in this manner is dramatic. A grandmother is an elder, a wise person, someone worthy of respect and caring. Referring to ayahuasca as a drug, or as simply a vine, would imply a different relationship. The process of using respectful and relational language to describe the natural world and its elements alters how people then relate to nature and the natural world. This sort of environmental ethos can be found in creation stories from Indigenous peoples all over the world. In these stories and myths, plants, animals, winds, the sun, and other natural elemental entities are depicted as teachers and relatives (Cajete, 1994; Iseke, 2013; Kovach, 2010). The depiction of the natural world as relatives and teachers affects how Indigenous peoples view the natural world, and therefore inspires these peoples to act with respect and care of the earth. This Indigenous sentiment regarding respect for the earth is well illustrated in the comments of Bolivian Foreign Minister David Choquehuanca (Vidal, 2011) regarding the role of Bolivia's traditional Indigenous respect for Pachachama, or Mother Earth:

> Our grandparents taught us that we belong to a big family of plants and animals. We believe that everything in the planet forms part of a big family. We Indigenous people can contribute to solving the energy, climate, food and financial crises with our values.

Comments About the Data. Eighty-two percent (9 out of 11) of survey participants reported some type of shift in how they relate to the natural world. Many participants who have worked with ayahuasca reported a shift towards viewing the natural world as sentient. The samples from the data demonstrate that, after working with ayahuasca, people report more reverence for the natural world, in particular, relating to the plant teacher ayahuasca as sentient. This reverence and appreciation also seems to extend towards having a greater appreciation for animals, the earth, and other plant species as well.

Antidote 3: Samples From the Data
-In ceremony I was connecting with plant and animal spirits directly (P2).
-When you connect with the plants you disconnect from greed, jealousy and anger (P5).
-I'm much more sympathetic about what is going on with Mother Earth (P3).
-When you really go deep with ayahuasca, you can't help but feel that ayahuasca has consciousness and really is a teacher and a healer (Ceremony Leader).
-These ceremonies connect us back to nature, to the natural world, because we are so removed from it (P10).
-Before ayahuasca, I never viewed plants as sentient beings that I could communicate with, or that had an independent consciousness (P4).
-Awe and reverence for nature (P7).
-I made a commitment to the plants (P10).
-I have learned about how the plant works, not that I even understand 1% of how it works (P2).
-Sentient, intelligent force in the plant medicine (P7).
-We are supposed to be one with Mother Earth, and plants, and everything. Until we walk that walk and let the plants teach us and help us understand that again, we are separate. (P5).

Antidote 3: Antidotal Movement Found in the Quantitative Data
On the question of consciousness of nonhumans, two statements were posed in the scaled survey:

Before taking ayahuasca, I thought that plants, animals, and nature have consciousness.

After taking ayahuasca, I thought that plants, animals, and nature have consciousness.

The table below shows that in both groups (participants who have worked with ayahuasca more than 50 times and participants who have worked with ayahuasca less than 50 times) move towards thinking that plants, animals, and nature have consciousness. Both groups show that after working with ayahuasca, 89%-90% agree or strongly agree that they thought plants, animals, and nature have consciousness. Both groups show a movement towards an anthropomorphic view.

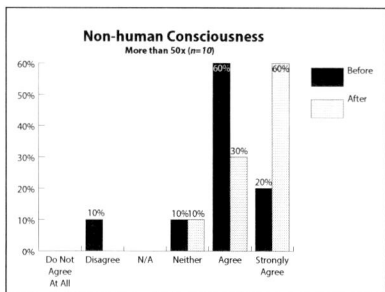 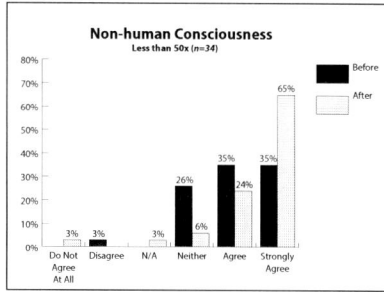

Comparison of connection to plants, animals, and the natural world: More than 50x ayahuasca versus less than 50x ayahuasca.

Discussion About Antidote 3

The data related to antidote 3 showed that 100% of the short qualitative interview participants noted a movement from anthropocentrism towards an anthropomorphic view of the natural world. Within the quantitative data, there was a large shift after the ayahuasca experience in beliefs about plants, animals, and nature having consciousness. This movement is even more pronounced in people who have worked with ayahuasca more than 50 times. This concept of relating to plant teachers and the natural world as sentient is an extension of Antidote 2, movement towards relationality. The data suggest that both qualitative and quantitative research participants moved towards relating to the natural world as sentient, and moved away from the Western hegemonic models that nature is subordinate to human beings. For example, an anonymous scaled questionnaire participant commented, "Ayahuasca changed my life. I thought I was already open-minded, but now feel much more so. It has made me feel more connected to people, animals, and nature. I think I am more empathetic now." The ayahuasca experience, in this case, helped this participant shift towards an anthropomorphic view of nature.

While the data suggest a shift in consciousness, such as the above comment from a research participant, it is unknown how those people who work with ayahuasca and who participated in the research studies have specifically changed their actions regarding being more focused on environmental sustainable or more respectful of the natural world. Do they consume less? Do they recycle more? Do they contribute money to environmental causes? Do they become politically active in environmental rights? Do they eat less meat or try to reduce their carbon footprint? How does this shift in consciousness change actions and not merely conceptual thought? Given the research questions and the parameters of my study, I do not have a way of answering this question.

Other Indigenous Ceremonies and Plant Medicines as Potential Antidotes. It is certainly likely that Westerners who participate in sweat lodges, Sun Dances, peyote ceremonies, and other forms of Indigenous ceremonies would also show a movement towards viewing the natural world as sentient. This shift, I assert, happens because those ceremonies and rituals are all grounded within an Indigenous worldview and are representational of this worldview. During sweat lodges, leaders often will give teachings about the importance of Mother Earth and the emphasis of human beings striving to live in harmony with nature. This sort of environmental ethos can be found in creation stories from Indigenous peoples all over the world. In these stories and myths plants, animals, winds, the sun, and other natural entities are depicted as teachers and relatives (Cajete, 1994; Iseke, 2013; Kovach, 2010).

Western-Academic Examples of Environmental Awareness. There have been some attempts in the academic world to describe the human-earth relationship in a way that honors the earth as sentient. This includes the "Gaia" theory, which is the idea that the earth is a self-regulating system and essentially alive (Sahtouris, 1989). The term "ecological awareness" is a concept from systems thinking that refers to ways in which everything is related, and all things influence each other (Wheatley, 1999, p. 158). Furthermore, the field of "ethno-ecology" proposes that bodies of knowledge exist between Indigenous cultures and their ecosystems (Martin, 2010). All of these definitions and fields of study draw influence from ancient Indigenous views of human relationships with the natural world and echo the Indigenous worldview, which is grounded in an anthropomorphic view of the natural world.

Environmental Protection Movements. There are many political protest movements that are focused on fostering environmental awareness and fighting institutional forms of environmental destruction. Groups like The Nature Conservancy are focused on protecting the earth and promoting environmental awareness. Some groups, like Earth First!, are more extreme and attempt to protect the earth using civil disobedience, grassroots organizing, and other forms of protest. There are many other organizations focused on environmental protection. While these organizations may be somewhat effective in affecting some change and environmental protection, they are not generally guided by and for Indigenous peoples or based on Indigenous spiritual principles.

On the other hand, Indigenous communities in every corner of the world are protesting environmental destruction, but within the context of an Indigenous worldview. Protesting in this case is tied to Indigenous values and priorities that position the environment and environmental issues as of utmost significance to communities, and therefore individuals. Cheyenne tribal member Gail Small has been successfully fighting to keep coal and other energy companies off Cheyenne lands. Small runs a non-profit, Native Justice, focusing on protecting the lands of Native peoples (Mihesuah, 2003; Native Action Org, 2012). Other tribal peoples throughout the United States have been vocal in the political arena to protest mining, pollution, "fracking," and other environmentally destructive practices. In 1993, Indigenous groups in Ecuador sued Chevron because of oil fields and pollution were contaminating Indigenous lands and affecting Indigenous peoples (Kimberling, 2005). From 2013 into 2014, the Indigenous people of Borneo protested the construction of several dams in their region (Davidson, 2014). As recently as 2013, the Sami people, primarily located in Norway and Sweden, were protesting a mine being built in Sweden because it would interfere and disrupt reindeer herds (Rising & Dougall, 2013). Since 2012, the Maori have been protesting American oil company Anadarko because of drilling off the west coast of New Zealand (Kaituhi, 2013). This is just a small sampling of Indigenous protest movements happening all over the world. All of these protest movements not only demonstrate models for civic engagement and acting to individually and communally protect the earth, but for community stewardship of the environment as well.

Indigenous ecological identities are interrelated because of intricate links between the cultural politics of the Indigenous movements and global environmental policies (Ulloa, 2013, p. 7).

Antidote 4:
Movement from Valuing Materialism and Consumerism Towards Meaning and Purpose Beyond these Structures

This antidote shows that after working with ayahuasca, participants move from a focus on materialism and consumerism towards finding meaning in other areas of life. Success in the West is unfortunately a zero-sum game, whereby some people succeed and some fail, and where there is a growing divide between rich and poor. The American dream is partially based on economic success, not on compassion, personal meaning, character, relational respect, nor any form of sustainable ethics, whereas ayahuasca ceremonies and ayahuasca culture centers around finding personal meaning within one's individual experience, and values self-sacrifice and compassion towards others as character traits.

Western Hegemonic Structure
Western hegemony and its incentive to profit from consumerism have been selling the myth of the "American dream," as exemplified by the cultural shift that occurred in the United States in the 1950s in a wave of post-World War II lifestyle changes. According to Derber (1979), the main component of the dream is that economic success and materialism are the driving forces in finding happiness. A potential implication of the American dream is not only that culture values related to valuing economic success over personal meaning, but that anyone can succeed if they simply work hard enough or pull themselves up by their own bootstraps. However, the notion that anyone can succeed is not true, nor is the notion that materialism causes happiness. These are myths that Western hegemony promotes to entice people into buying more products and create stratification.

Returning again to the hegemonic structures that hold commodification and materialism in place, Western hegemony pushes the idea that everything can be seen as a commodity, including activities, knowledge, and social relationships (Bowers, 2000, p. 74). American cultural paradigms tend to view human beings, cultures, and the natural world exclusively through the filter of their commodity value. Therefore, nearly everything in the West is reduced to its value in the marketplace (Welton, 1995). In the process, advertisers and hegemons, who, in turn, drive Western views, promote the idea that happiness can only be found in materialism. This Western hegemonic process exists so that large-scale institutions can profit. Harms and Kellner (1991) explain one component of the process:

> advertising should be seen as an indispensible force in the reproduction of consumer capitalism and in the maintenance of capitalist hegemony. Indeed, advertising has multi-faceted social functions, ranging from short-range efforts to induce individuals to buy specific products to more long range functions that attempt to sell consumer capitalism as a way of life. (p. 3)

The view of profit and commodification is flawed on many levels, however. Consumer capitalism only works for the wealthy, not for the poor. While the wealthy can buy anything they want, the poor cannot keep up. This distinctly Western view creates a situation where everyone is constantly trying to gain more financial success and hardly have any time to contemplate their life or find meaning in any other areas of life.

Antidotal Movement

This antidotal movement happens as ayahuasca users move from viewing external factors, such as materialism, career status, and financial success, as the sole indicators of happiness and fulfillment, toward looking at more relational realms, such as the spiritual, sacred, and kinship-based, to frame meaning and purpose. This movement towards rejecting materialism as the main focus of life is part of an Indigenous worldview. Four Arrows and Narvaez (2014) propose that elements of the Indigenous worldview include socially purposeful living, community involvement and social support, valuing generosity, and recognition of the Great Spirit in everything. While these elements do not describe a precise antidote per se, they show how Indigenous peoples move away from the trappings of viewing every aspect of life as a commodity, and find purpose outside of commodification and materialism. This is not to romanticize Indigenous peoples or a time in the distant past before technology, but these models present a map to avoid some of the trappings of Western hegemony by operating with a different set of assumptions and a different worldview.

Another element of advice Indigenous wisdom addresses for living outside of the hegemonic structures of consumerism and materialism is through experiential and emotional learning models. Deloria and Wildcat (2001) offer a key distinction from Indigenous wisdom to understanding the significance of experiential learning, they argue that the Indigenous response to Descartes' assertion, "I think therefore I am" is, "I experience, therefore I am" (p. 148). As a contrast to Western models, Indigenous learning and meaning involves cultivation of one's senses, such as how to deeply listen, observe, and experience things holistically (Cajete, 1994). The Indigenous model suggests that sacredness in daily life is felt through direct experiences and direct actions (Deloria, & Wildcat, 2001). These Indigenous views on the significance of direct experience and experiential learning support the notion that the ayahuasca experience can be extremely powerful and transformative for those who work with it in a ceremonial context. One of the essential ways in which meaning is constructed within Indigenous models and forms of knowledge is through creative acts. Creativity may take the form of making sacred art, songs, dances, storytelling, prayer, ritual, play, or through reflection (Cajete, 1994, p. 42). Perhaps the Indigenous proposition that creativity is a gateway to meaning is a useful way to bypass materialism and consumerism. When someone is having direct experiences based on creativity, he or she does not necessarily require material goods or economic success to dictate fulfillment. These Indigenous examples of creativity suggest models of meaning that are outside of Western hegemonic models of materialism, and operate within an entirely different paradigm. My qualitative data show that people move away from some of the trappings of consumerism and materialism towards a different meaning schema, as put forth in the Indigenous worldview.

Comments about the Data. Eighty-two percent (nine out of eleven) of the qualitative interview participants reported a shift in how they view materialism, commodification, and the role of career after working with ayahuasca. While earlier antidotes include a discussion about commodification and its hegemonic influence, participants note their priorities move away from Western hegemonic influences.

ANTIDOTE 4: SAMPLES FROM THE DATA
-The work I do now is important enough and makes me happy to be doing it and that has a greater value to me than making more money (P6).
-I live simply and don't have a lot of stuff, nor do I want a lot of stuff (P2).
-Before the medicine, I thought I always had to have like this career and a lot of money (P4).

- I think once I started working with the medicine, I realized that the whole way of thinking was not where I needed to be (being career-focused and making more money). (P5).
-Anecdotally, it seems that people who use medicine tend to be less materialistically attached (P8).
-Before, I was more likely to get comfort from material goods. Now it doesn't matter (P7).
-I look at how I spend my money differently (P2).
-Early on, the Grandmother had me re-think my whole life and my priorities. Working with the medicine had me walk away from my career and stop focusing so hard on making money, and accumulating so much "stuff." Instead I started living more simply and changed my focus to trying to help people heal their lives (Ceremony Leader).
-Ayahuasca helped me relate to my professional and financial situations with less attachment to the outcome and to spend less energy on these things (P4).
-People associated with the medicine path have the approach to living life in a light, unattached way regarding belongings (P8).
-It changed my focus to be more of a healer, and not just a corporate slave (P7).
-Lost the drive to make more money and get a better position at the company (P10).
-Removed material bonds—because they weigh you down (P6).

ANTIDOTE 4: ANTIDOTAL MOVEMENT FOUND IN THE QUANTITATIVE DATA

On the question of the importance of material goods, two statements were posed in the scaled questionnaire:

Before taking ayahuasca, buying and having many material possessions was very important to me.
After taking ayahuasca, having material possessions is less meaningful to me.

The next figure shows a shift in participants away from materialism after working with ayahuasca. It is interesting that the group that has worked with ayahuasca more than 50 times shows that, before working with ayahuasca, 70% disagreed or did not agree at all that having material possessions was important to them; after working with ayahuasca, 90% reported that having material possessions is less important to them. Whereas, in the group that has worked with ayahuasca less than 50 times, 50%

agree or strongly agree that, before working with ayahuasca, buying and having many material possessions was important to them. In the group that has worked with ayahuasca more than 50 times, only 20% agreed or strongly agreed that, before working with ayahuasca, buying and having many material possessions was important to them. In the group that has worked with ayahuasca less than 50 times, 64% agree or strongly agree that having material possessions is less important after working with ayahuasca. Both charts show a movement away from materialism after the ayahuasca experience.

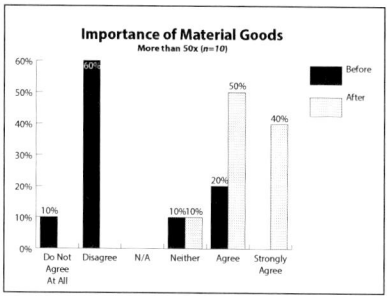 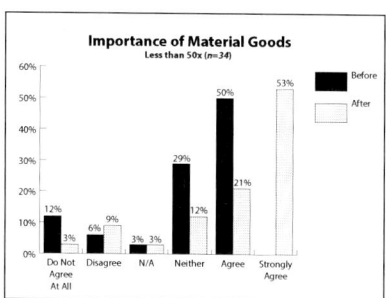

Comparision of having material posessions and their meaning: More than 50x ayahuasca versus less than 50x ayahuasca.

DISCUSSION ABOUT ANTIDOTE 4

Throughout each step of my research for this book, I became more aware of the destructive forces of Western hegemony, especially commodification and consumerism. These forms of Western hegemony attempt to reduce people, places, and things down to an economic value. This dynamic of always looking to profit, without any concern for the cost or the price paid by people, nature, or the impact on future generations, seems to be one of the central problems with Western hegemony. This push towards consumption is what inspired me to explore hegemony more deeply and, perhaps, work towards finding potential antidotes that could be executed in a realistic manner. A connected theme to consumerism, which is embedded in American culture, is the notion that material success results in happiness. As a result, my research on the ayahuasca experience, in particular the antidotes to Western hegemony, looks for a sense of meaning and purpose outside of materialism and consumerism.

Indigenous cosmologies do not necessarily address issues related to consumerism and materialism. The Indigenous worldview, however stresses generosity as a value, while the Western worldview supports selfishness and accumulation. The Western worldview supports individuals envisioning their "legacy" to be money given to their children, while the Indigenous worldview values someone living with high character to pass on values to his or her children. These guideposts suggest a disparity in values regarding cultural aims and views on consumption. Part of the solution to this problem may be to look at ways to disengage from consumerism.

It seems as if Western hegemons propose the idea that the purpose of life is a never-ending accumulation of wealth. In 2014, billionaire Mark Cuban said, "Business is my morning meditation" (Shandrow, 2014). Cuban's comments demonstrate a belief that suggests business and economic success are more important than personal meaning and/or spiritual meaning as the driving force in one's life. His comments are ironic in that some people wake up and meditate on peace or welfare for all, while Cuban's meditation is on money and business. To Cuban and others who may share his set of values, consumerism and materialism become the driving purpose and frame the meaning of life, even though there is significant evidence to show that the division between those who have wealth and those who do not continues to widen, and the increase in consumptive patterns is not environmentally sustainable. Cuban's comments demonstrate how hegemony infuses the values and beliefs of many people in the West away from Indigenous values and an Indigenous worldview.

American Trends Against Consumerism. There are trends within American culture to fight against consumerism, a push that seems to move away from the insatiable drive for "retail therapy" and "shop til you drop" mentalities. The 1999 film Fight Club (Bell & Fincher) put forth a storyline about the disenchantment with American consumerism. This quotation articulates some of the frustration of a generation fed up with the push towards consumerism:

Advertising has us chasing cars and clothes, working jobs we hate so we can buy shit we don't need. We're the middle children of history, man. No purpose or place. We have no Great War. No Great Depression. Our Great War's a spiritual war... our Great Depression is our lives. We've all been raised on television to believe that one day we'd all be millionaires, and movie gods, and rock stars. But we won't.

The same sentiment can be found in a number of anti-consumerism trends in American over the past decade. The ayahuasca experience may act as a galvanizing experience, whereby people find personal meaning outside of consumerism and change their lives to move away from the influences of hegemony. Whereas, people may already have made a decision to downsize their lives or attempt to live in a less materialistic manner, as suggested by the small housing movement, also knowns as the tiny house movement, those who work with ayahuasca may realize on a more existential level that they no longer wish to participate in consumerism or no longer need or require as many material possessions as they previously thought.

Antidote 5:
Movement from Acceptance of Western Hegemonic Institutions Towards Criticality or Rejection

This antidote shows a movement in participants who work with ayahuasca from accepting the influence of Western institutions such as the American political system, media, Western academia, Western medicine, and the effects of colonization and globalization toward rejecting these institutions and moving toward a position of criticality; and, in some cases, an all-out rejection of these systems, leading to nonparticipation. Ayahuasca ceremony participants, without being steeped in the works of Freire or academic models of learning, seem to move towards the development of critical consciousness from their participation in ayahuasca ceremonies.

Western Hegemonic Structure
Four Arrows (2006) explains, "The term [hegemony] thus signifies the ability of the dominant social leaders to cultivate, through largely non-coercive means, a popular worldview that naturalizes their positions in a way that manipulates subordinate classes of people to consent to their own subordination and oppression, thinking that it ultimately serves their best interests" (p. 27).According to Herman and Chomsky (2008), "The media serve, and propagandize on behalf of, the powerful societal interests that control and finance them" (p. xi). These powerful social interests include political groups and large corporations. Herman and Chomsky (2008) later suggest that one of the major ingredients in the U.S. propaganda model includes, "The reliance of the media on information provided by government, business, and "experts" funded and approved by these primary sources and agents of power" (p. 2).

Within the framework of American politics, a small elite group of people holds the power, while the masses have very little input. This system is highly influenced by the institutions that have the most money, such as the banking system, corporations, media giants, and investment firms. These institutions, which are led by a small number of people, then influence government. In response to pressure, the government, which appears to be corrupted by a small number of hegemons, only makes incremental changes, if any changes at all, in public policy (Schubert, Dye, & Zeigler, 2015, p. 13). In other words, hegemony, in this case, relates to the concepts first articulated by Gramsci as, "the process by which ruling elites secure consent to the established political order through the production and diffusion of meanings and values" (Carragee & Roefs 2004, pp. 221-222).

Four Arrows (2010) describes how Western hegemonic institutions use fear as a mechanism to control people and keep them trapped into not questioning the influence of Western hegemony:

> In Western tradition, authority stems generally from external sources. We listen to the authority of our books, our teachers, our preachers, our parents, our leaders, etc. Such authority, especially when coupled with fear or stress, literally hypnotizes us to believe the messages of the authority figure, no matter how incorrect. To the contrary, Indigenous wisdom teaches that the only true source of authority is personal reflection, honest reflection, on lived experience in light of the spiritual understanding that everything is connected. (p. 26)

Within most models of Western academia, Western epistemological concepts drive a biased view of what is considered valid in areas such as culture, education, knowledge, language, social relationships, law, and scholarship (Blaut, 1993; Ermine, Sinclair & Jeffrey, 2004; Smith, 1999). Ladson-Billings (2003) asserts that the Western epistemological approach pervades the (academic) academy (p. 402). Eurocentric ways of operating dictate which methods are employed and which are not; which methods and traditions are heralded as significant, and those that are marginalized. Grande (2008) concludes that (Western) institutions, scholarship, vocabulary, and doctrines all support Western discourse, and by extension, institutional forms of Western hegemony.

ANTIDOTAL MOVEMENT

Indigenous peoples can teach Western people how to move away from Western hegemonic structures entirely and recreate systems anew. According to Smith (1999), "One of the strategies that Indigenous peoples have employed effectively to bind people together politically is a strategy which asks that people imagine a future, that they rise above present day situations which are generally depressing, dream a new dream, and set a new vision" (p. 152). Cajete (1994) also discusses "visioning", but in the context of Indigenous educational models. Visioning, he asserts, becomes a source of empowerment (p. 209). Smith's teachings on the purpose of dreaming a new dream and setting a new vision is akin to Cajete's discussion on the role visioning has within Indigenous educational models. The ayahuasca experience and its ability to give people actual "visions" during the ayahuasca ceremonies, along with offering new perspectives at looking at life, give ayahuasca ceremony participants the opportunity to create entire new systems outside of the influence of Western hegemony.

One way to move away from these destructive Western hegemonic forces is to develop criticality, or to even reject Western hegemonic institutions altogether. One powerful model of developing criticality can be found within the work of critical pedagogy. Ira Shor (1993) proposes that Freirean education is based on developing critical consciousness. As part of the process, individuals go through "de-socialization." Shor describes this process as:

> Recognizing and challenging the myths, values, behaviors, and language learned in mass culture; critically examining the regressive values operating in society, which are internalized into consciousness such as racism, sexism, class bias, homophobia, a fascination with the rich and powerful, hero-worship, excess consumerism, run away individualism, militarism, and national chauvinism. (p. 32)

One of the central problems with the Western hegemony is its influence on the political system. Alfred (1999) describes some of the differences between Western hegemonic governance models and Indigenous models this way:

> Indigenous governance systems embody distinctive political values, radically different from those of the mainstream. Western notions of domination (human and natural) are noticeably absent; in their place we find harmony, autonomy, and respect. We have a responsibility to recover, understand, and preserve these values, not only because they represent a unique contribution to the history of ideas, but because renewal of respect for traditional values is the only lasting solution to the political, economic, and social problems that beset our people. (p. 5)

Indigenous systems of democracy mostly are mostly rooted in Indigenous values. Indigenous values strive towards participation, inclusivity, and consensus-based decision-making. This model encourages, for instance, leaders to have a council of elders for input in making decisions. This model also encourages local-level political autonomy. I am not mentioning this model to suggest that some Indigenous groups operate without corruption, but that Indigenous political models do exist and are quite different in structure and in the values they promote, compared to Western models. This Indigenous-based political model presents one path to combat hegemony.

Another example of criticality and challenging Western hegemonic institutions can be seen in Indigenous protest movements happening in every corner of the globe. These forms of protest and criticality highlight a movement away from a Western model of politics and governance towards more sustainable models of social and political life. Indigenous peoples have been at the forefront of human rights movements and the environmental justice movement. For instance, in 2012, a group of Indigenous Canadian women formed the Idle No More Movement to protest several Canadian bills giving the government more control over land usage, which would result in more corporate access to waterways. These bills would likely result in an increase in toxic pollution and environmental degradation. The Idle No More Movement quickly became a worldwide Indigenous rights and environmental rights movement, and mobilized many Indigenous peoples to become more politically active (Bernd, 2013; Idle No More, 2013). Certainly, the American Indian Movement (AIM) is another example of a politically rooted Indigenous social change movement, created to bring about self-determination for American Indian peoples and American Indian legal rights.

Comments about the Data. Seventy-three percent (8 out of 11) of short interview participants reported an increase in political awareness, criticality of Western institutions, and/or a shift in their choices to participate or not participate within the framework of politics and other hegemonic institutions.

ANTIDOTE 5: SAMPLES FROM THE DATA
-*If politicians used ayahuasca, they would care less about ego and power (P5).*
-*It makes you more sensitive and more aware of what is going on in the world. And that doesn't go away. It has a lasting effect. (P3).*

-I have found that over time, I am much more involved and intrigued by what is happening in my immediate area politically, much more than before the medicine (P4).

-Before the medicine, I was thinking of politics on a more worldly scale, but now it's more about my immediate surroundings. With the medicine, I've realized there is not a whole lot I can accomplish in a worldly way, but, from a local place, I can bring about change and affect people. I'm also just more interested in what is happening locally (P6).

-It has helped me to see a broader perspective, to be more critical, discerning, and understanding whether it's local politics or when people are arguing (P4).

-I guess I'm apolitical now, since doing the medicine (P1).

-Political movements are part of the "against" model of the world. From an ayahuasca perspective, you are looking at being free from the whole trap of Westernization. We are trying to help people be liberated from themselves, their culture, their history, towards self-determination for themselves and the entire planet (Ceremony Leader).

-Politically, I've given up on politics (P4).

-I ignore politics because it is so screwed up (P10).

-More socially aware, but I don't follow what is going on (P9).

-You see injustices more, and the way the status quo has set up the world (P7).

-After ayahuasca, some people become more politically active or want to become healers (P7).

-I'm apathetic to politics (P10).

-You feel from ayahuasca that you have the support to be courageous in life and stop injustice (P7).

-The medicine made my commitment to social justice and caring for people stronger (P6).

-Put me in touch with oppression (P10).

-I felt a strong sense of empathy of the effects of oppression and exploitation (P3).

-Aware of what it's like when people take advantage of others for their resources (P3).

-The whole political scheme is dysfunctional. All these egos (P5).

-Politicians are destroying our lives and destroying Pachamama, and destroying everything (P5). [Note: the Indigenous Andean people refer to the Mother of the World and the Mother Goddess as Pachamama.]

Antidote 5: Antidotal Movement Found in the Quantitative Data

On the question of acting in response to injustice, two statements were posed in the scaled questionnaire:

Before ayahuasca, I try to intervene when there is injustice.
After ayahuasca, I am more likely to intervene when there is injustice.

This statement points to the hegemonic structure of the oppressive forces of injustice; as a result, I am drawing a connection between injustice on an institutional level and intervening on behalf of injustice as a form of criticality expressed in action. This points to a movement away from simply accepting Western hegemonic forces and taking an active role to change or intervene. The following figure regarding injustice, shows that the group of participants that has worked with ayahuasca more than 50 times show a much larger movement towards intervening when there is injustice than those who have worked with ayahuasca less than 50 times. Of the group of participants that has worked with ayahuasca more than 50 times, 100% agree or strongly agree that they are more likely to intervene when there is injustice. The group of participants that has worked with ayahuasca less than 50 times shows that 50% agree or strongly agree that they are more likely to intervene when there is injustice after working with ayahuasca.

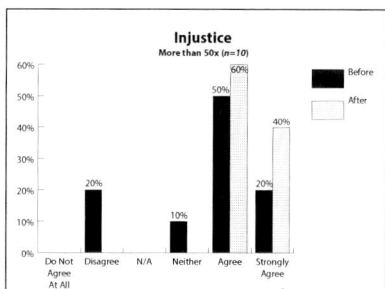 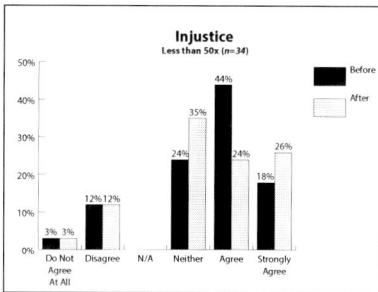

Comparison intervening when there is injustice: More than 50x ayahuasca versus less than 50x ayahuasca.

On the question of political action, two questions were asked:

Before taking ayahuasca, I was politically active.
After taking ayahuasca, my level of political action changed.

This figure shows that, among the participants that have worked with ayahuasca more than 50 times, 70% agree that their level of political action changed after taking ayahuasca. The group of participants that has experienced ayahuasca fewer than 50 times show a much more distributed response when asked whether their level of political action has changed since taking ayahuasca, including a large number of the participants disagreeing or strongly disagreeing (39%) that their level of political action has changed at all. The group that has worked with ayahuasca more than 50 times shows a much bigger change after working with ayahuasca than those who have worked with ayahuasca less than 50 times.

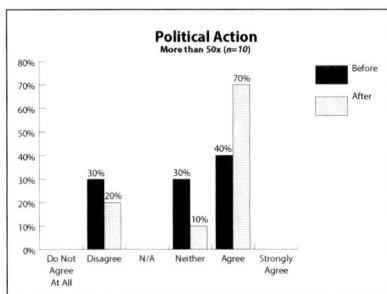 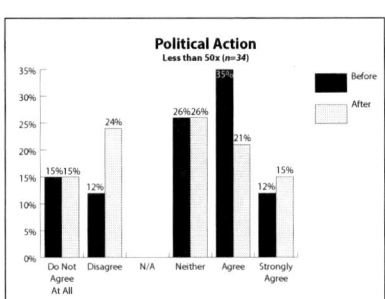

Comparision of political action: More than 50x ayahuasca versus less than 50x ayahuasca

On the question of social awareness two statements were posed in the scaled questionnaire:

Before taking ayahuasca, I was socially aware.
After taking ayahuasca, social awareness was more important to me.

Social awareness is another area related to criticality. The following figure shows that, of the participants who have worked with ayahuasca more than 50 times, 90% agree or strongly agree that social awareness was more important to them after working with ayahuasca. At the same time, 80% agreed or strongly agreed that social awareness was important to them before working with ayahuasca. So, there was a 10% increase in agreeing or strongly agreeing about the importance of social awareness after working with ayahuasca. With the participants who have worked with ayahuasca less than 50 times, 74% agreed or strongly agreed that social awareness was important to them before working with ayahuasca, and 70% agree or strongly agree that social awareness was important to them after working with ayahuasca. In other words, it appears that there was a decrease in the importance of social awareness in people who worked with ayahuasca less than 50 times, not an increase.

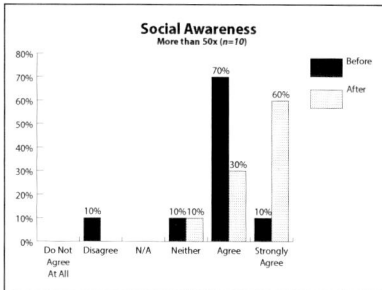 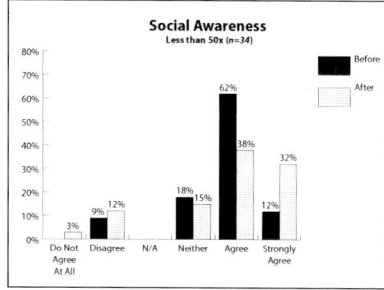

Comparison of social awareness: More than 50x ayahuasca versus less than 50x ayahuasca.

Discussion About Antidote 5

I had assumed that people who participate in ayahuasca ceremonies might be more politically active after working with ayahuasca than before working with it. I was surprised, however, to find that many participants in the short qualitative interviews commented that they were now apolitical or did not follow politics, or had simply given up on politics. P5 argued, "The whole political scheme is dysfunctional. All these egos." In fact, 64% of the qualitative interview subjects reported giving up on politics or rejecting the political system altogether. My quantitative research data suggested that 70% of people who have worked with ayahuasca more than 50 times reported a change in political action. Social awareness is another area related to criticality. Of the participants in the quantitative scaled questionnaire who worked with ayahuasca more than 50 times, 90% agree or strongly agree that social awareness was more important to them after working with ayahuasca. These trends were interesting because at the same time, some of the qualitative interviews suggested an increase in engagement on a smaller more localized scale. P4, who in the interview suggested, "Politically, I've given up on politics," also reported fighting to have fluoride removed in his city's water system, along with other examples of civic participation. P6 also mentioned being more active on a local level: "Before the medicine I was thinking of politics on a more worldly scale, but now it's more about my immediate surroundings. With the medicine I've realized there is not a whole lot I can accomplish in a worldly way, but from a local place I can bring about change and affect people." In addition, one of the quantitative scaled survey participants commented,

> I am more politically aware, but less angry about what I see. I was very politically active when Scott Walker started making changes with Wisconsin, and went daily to protests. Now, I feel that the best work I can do may not be from standing in a crowd of people in front of a news camera pointed the other way, but to act from love as much as possible, because it seems that nothing can change the world more than love.

One of the ways in which I interpret the data and this trend towards being apolitical and ceasing to engage in the political system after ayahuasca usage is that perhaps people turn away from the entire hegemonic system of politics and its inherent polarization and oppressive quality. Given that political change happens slowly, if at all, and can often seem corrupt, perhaps this antidotal movement is a demonstration of simply disengaging from this structure and rejecting it entirely to move toward a different way of focusing on smaller level politics and social issues.

Democratization. A theme related to criticality, found within critical pedagogy, is democracy and supporting democratization. Hooks (2003) argues that mass-based political movements calling on citizens to uphold democracy and the rights of everyone to be educated, to work on behalf of ending domination in all of its forms are needed. In particular, she suggests that the education system needs to be changed to fight against "imperialist white-supremacist capitalist patriarchy or any ideology" (p. 3). Shor (1992) asserts that all forms of education are, by definition, political. They are political in the way they enable or inhibit discussion, questioning, and reflection on knowledge, school, and society. These models of criticality imply a movement either toward the encouragement of actual democracy, which would imply an educated model of political engagement, or developing more awareness of the challenges of democracy and the ways in which hegemony prevents authentic democracy from occurring, through the tendency to create obstacles to real information that can inform democratic participation.

Critical theory aims to encourage democracy, and examines ways in which the American model of democracy is not really a democracy. For example, in his discussion about critical theory, Farr (2009) argues that a society may not be a democracy because, "There are members of society who do not have proper access to education and necessary cultural, social, and economic resources for the kind of self-development and self-determination needed for democratic participation" (p. 124). Farr (2009) mentions a second obstacle to democratic participation—the lack of information, rather than the "proliferation of useless, administered, manipulative information" (p. 124). Neoliberal capitalism, Giroux and Giroux (2008) argue, is "wedded to the belief that the market should be the organizing principle for all political, social and economic decisions" (p. 182). This force of neoliberalism is in contrast to democracy and democratic values. If neoliberal capitalism, rather than democracy for the sake of community involvement, is the driving force of politics, then we do not have an actual democracy. While these descriptions of the various forces of Western hegemony seem accurate, they do not include solutions to these problems, whereas the ayahuasca experience seems to point to more concrete models for change.

Self-Determination. One way to combat the hegemonic forces of neoliberal capitalism is the Indigenous notion of self-determination. Self-determination is a theme found within Indigenous literature, and is relevant to a discussion about freedom and democracy. Self-determination, in this case, does not refer to individual freedom the same way it is defined in Antidote 1: movement from the personal trappings of Western hegemony towards self-determination, but towards self-determination on a more political and cultural level. In discussing what self-determination might look like for the Maori people of New Zealand, Bishop (2008) explains, that self-determination "seeks to operationalize the Maori people's aspirations to restructure power relationships to the point where partners can be autonomous and interact from this position, rather than one from subordination or dominance" (p. 440). Bishop also contrasts Indigenous views of self-determination with Western views of self-determination, highlighting that the Western view focuses on territoriality that coincides to sovereignty over a space or a people. In contrast, the Indigenous views of self-determination are relational, acknowledge interdependence, and encourage peoples to make sense of the world in their own culturally generated manner (p. 440). Self-determination is one of the key themes in my research on the antidotal movements away from Western hegemony.

Critique of Critical Pedagogy. Some challenges with the approaches to criticality and political awareness that are presented by critical pedagogy, including Hooks, are that they seem to suggest it is necessary to learn about democratization in the classroom, or in a formalized manner. Furthermore, the assumption also seems to be that the notion of criticality itself is necessary. At the same time, it seems that what critical pedagogy refers to as "criticality" is conceived of and based in a Western model of critical thinking. Perhaps in a Utopian sense, if an Indigenous community were not exposed to corruption and hegemony in the same way that Western culture is, developing criticality might not even be necessary. At the same time, it seems as though the Western model of criticality may project the image of the noble savage onto Indigenous communities, such as those in South America who work with ayahuasca, with the assumption being these Indigenous peoples are uneducated and have nothing to offer in terms of promoting criticality.

Perhaps the Indigenous peoples who work with ayahuasca have, in their own way, consciously turned away from the influences of Western hegemony by making a series of choices to live simply and to find political awareness and take action on a personal level, not as a grand demonstration. Maybe, from their perspective, it is evident that Western models of politics are corrupt and destructive and the solution is to disengage from these forms of hegemony. Perhaps, rather than focus on development of criticality on an intellectual level, the ayahuasca communities in South America have developed heightened somatic awareness and are able to feel corruption and the forces of hegemony on a visceral-level, and the potential solution to hegemony is viewed as an issue best addressed though visceral-level change on an individual level, not on a large political scale. I am not pretending to know what Indigenous people feel about criticality or democratization. I cannot possibly know what various different groups and individuals feel about a particular topic, but I can suggest that the Western model is incomplete and only presents one worldview and one perspective on a complicated issue.

Michael Yellowbird interview, September 22, 2015

I was glad that Michael Yellowbird agreed to be part of the book, due to his background in American Indian Studies and teaching critical thinking to tribal peoples, along with his research background in decolonizing methodologies, and how this may apply to fostering criticality in people. Dr. Yellowbird, Ph.D., is a citizen of the three affiliated tribes, (Mandan, Hidatsa, and Arikara). He is currently a professor and Director of the Tribal Indigenous Studies program at North Dakota State University. His teaching, writing, research, and community work focus on Indigenous Peoples' health, leadership, and cultural rights; the effects of colonization and methods of decolonization; decolonizing social work approaches; decolonizing war and military service; neurodecolonization and mind-body approaches. He is has written widely on decolonization and Indigenous peoples.

So when you were writing about starting critical thinking centers, how is that an Indigenous way of thinking, or a pedagogical model?

Michael Yellowbird: Yeah, when I actually wrote that piece, I was actually doing a lot of work on looking at the process of critical thinking, kind of more as a process than an act that all people do. Yet, the idea behind it is that Indigenous people under colonialism were not given or are given much less ability to think critically about their circumstances and their situations, and how their lives are affected by different aspects of colonialism to the point where they are often depressed in response to the racism, denial and isolation. Of course, the volume after volume that speaks down to the culture as being primitive and backwards and not having any redeeming values or contributions to human civilization, and so on, only makes matters worse.

Those things are all very much grounded in whole kind of colonial framework of oppression. The colonial framework created boarding schools and policies, and became sort of the lynchpin that helped hold Indigenous people in some kind of intellectual servitude to depend upon a colonizer to think for you and tell you how to think. As a result, Indigenous people couldn't think critically or question the colonizers' motives or their history or the contribution, certainly they didn't fit into the framework, or they weren't allowed to be part of the discourse in civilization.

So, I thought, that's interesting to think about how colonized our thought and our thinking processes have become. I don't remember if I talked about this in the critical thinking paper that

    I wrote about, how a lot of times we outsource our thinking. It's not only Indigenous people who are colonized by these other bodies—politics, or economics, or culture, to think in a particular way, and not to think beyond a particular way. Religion is a big one for it. When I went to Catholic boarding school, got a good education, a colonial education. Coming from Civil Rights Movement and anti-Vietnam War stuff, human rights. However, there was this area that we could not think critically about, and that was religion. We could not question religion. We had to outsource our thinking to the priests and to the nuns and to the Church.

    That is what has happened to Native people in a lot of ways after a period of colonization, they outsource—outsource it to white intellectuals, anthropologists, bureaucrats, spiritual people, Christians, whatever. The idea was to develop tribal critical thinking centers that would enable people to examine that history of colonization, intellectual colonization, so they could begin to decolonize that whole intellectual tradition and that oppression of that intellectual paradigm that exists in the world by first examining, what were people's motives for not letting them think or be part of this larger discourse of humanity? Then to begin to look at their own histories in depth, to find out the intellectual innovations, ideas, beliefs, technologies that they had that made sense to them at that time. It is often argued that Indigenous people didn't discover the wheel, so they are very primitive. Of course that's not true. They discovered the whole concept of wheel. They used them in toys, and they used them in different kinds of instruments and stuff. They never used it for draft animals that were domesticated because they did not have any. The idea is that the whole anthropological discipline, along with other disciplines, said this is a defining feature of these people—they are primitive, they never discovered the wheel.

    So, I want people to think about that, to discover all these innovations and intellectual traditions of their particular people, how they were able to manifest different kinds and ways of thought in order to survive climate change, genocide, droughts, intertribal warfare, diseases, and all these traditions were clearly there, intellectually. How were they able to develop a whole civilization, and towns, and cities, and were able to hunt and gather in ways that were way beyond our thinking of what hunting and gathering is? They were able to identify certain kinds of plants, and tubers, and certain kinds of berries. This whole process of empirical study of the landscapes, and animals, and people, and the climate, and so on, those intellectual traditions are there.

Now, interestingly enough, it seems to me, a lot of it is coming back now because of climate change. People are looking to Indigenous people's knowledge about how did you survive climate change, what did you eat, what did you do, how did your political systems function, how did you socially construct your society to adopt one another in order to create a more tightknit collective society in order to try to get these human-driven or natural climate change things, or war, whatever it was? So those traditions are there.

I just want people in tribal critical thinking centers to examine all these aspects of it and begin to come away and say, oh, yeah, people knew what they were doing, made a lot of sense for the times they were living in. And they were living at the apex of their society whenever they needed to be. They also need to understand that new fused ideas that come from diverse sources. Their society or any society will go stagnant unless they are able to adapt. This is clearly what Indigenous people have done, is they have been able to adapt. So, that's what's going on now. It's not so much that we are assimilated, not so much that we are colonized. But to understand that we have thoughtfully adapted to the changing conditions, then, I think people will have a very different viewpoint of themselves as Indigenous people.

Is that more akin to a Freire idea of being aware of one's oppression, which is, in some ways, applicable to what I've been looking at, is how do we become aware of that oppression and what process do we have to go through, even as, like, a white guy? We are in this culture that is incredibly oppressive and is hegemonic. There are all these implicit assumptions that drive us with consumerism.

MY: Oppression – in order to decolonize, one has to understand various levels of oppression, self-imposed oppression, internal, external. One has to be able to name them and then begin to look at themselves to figure out, how does that oppression apply to me on a daily basis? So, in order to decolonize, we have to understand that, and then begin to take steps and actions toward decolonizing how we are embedded or have internalized that kind of internal colonialism or racism or oppression. But, it's hard to understand, I think, unless you go through this period of decolonization, and you really understand what colonization is all about. So, that is the really important thing of the tribal critical thinking centers. People come to really understand colonialism from a number of different viewpoints. It could be social, political, economic, colonialism, and specifically, what grounds colonialism in the sense that it relates to me as a person, as an individual.

A model that I like to use now, that I have not really written about, is taking a look at colonialism in the sense of the microbial world. Colonialism has different viruses or different bacteria that can invade the body. But, as long as you've got enough good bacteria or good viruses operating in your system, got good bacteria in your gut, that's a big thing in the world today. The bad bacteria can't really create different kinds of gastrointestinal diseases, like Crohn's Disease or irritable bowel syndrome, IBS, and all these different kinds of things that then lead to colon cancer. The same idea goes with people and colonization. The idea is, if there are lots of viruses coming into society, as long as you've got healthy viruses, or thoughts, or intellectual traditions, these other viruses can be neutralized by that. That's a way to look at colonialism in another way, is that being invaded by these ideas, beliefs, values, like consumerism. What is the context of it? What's the fallout from having too much of this bad bacteria in your brain or your gut or your metabolic processes? Once the bad bacteria sort of overcomes the good bacteria, then you have a collapse in your system, your body, your processes collapse, and then other diseases begin to take over, and get cancer and heart disease, and that all leads to death.

I'm trying to use a model that can help people understand that colonialism is so simple, it comes in an idea and people believe those ideas, but it's ideas that have an overwhelming sort of capacity to overrun your ideas and your belief system about consumerism, for instance. This is the other idea of the tribal critical thinking center is that colonialism has to be put in all these different paradigms and studied in that particular kind of way, so that people say, "I got it now. I understand what colonialism is in all these different contexts."

In my opinion, a lot of people, colleagues included, have not really come down to a point where they understand it is not just something that happens, but it is something that happens much like an invasion of a foreign bacteria. We still have these ideas within us, it's like the bad bacteria, but the good bacteria gets overwhelmed by the bad stuff, and then the collapse and breakdown or a change that happens in the organism. So, we can live with so many ideas, like so much bad bacteria, and the more it builds up the more breakdown that happens to the body, to the person, to the culture, to the belief system. I don't know if that is making any sense, it makes perfect sense to me.

No, it makes sense, but it also seems like a function of time that most people, Indigenous or not, don't want to put in the time or rigor. Like for me in my Master's program, I used to throw the Pedagogy of the Oppressed book against the wall because I was like, this doesn't make any sense. These words and concepts seemed so complicated. It takes a lot of time to let these ideas sink in, or even hegemony in action.

MY: You are right. I think that's what it is. The whole term he came up with is "conscientization," it's kind of like the "aha" experience of colonialism. It is like drinking tap water. There's such a thing called body burden related to chemicals, and heavy metals, and pesticides, inorganic things in water do a lot of damage to your body. After years and years, you end up with a bald spot on your head. You've got really high levels of copper in your system and your hair falling out, and if your copper gets any higher you're going to start having circulatory problems. I'm drinking tap water, and they tell me it's good for me to drink, and the EPA says it's good. Then there are these crazy people out there saying the water is poison. They are ready to smash up these water filtration plants because they add chemicals to our water, and its polluting our clean water. The water is already polluted, but that's the idea.

I think we all just go with what we are told, unless we get these "aha" moments, which lead us to wonder, why would they add fluoride to the water? It does nothing for us. Well, there's a whole company, DuPont, which is one of the old family money, along with like Vanderbilts and all these super-rich, elite, old money people that sell fluoride to all the public water systems. They also control the EPA and everybody else, so they can say that we all have to have fluoride in the water system. Everyone then believes it, all of a sudden they are poisoning us, and we didn't realize that. That's the "aha" moment of conscientization that Friere talks about.

I think that is really apparent in colonization. Follow the money trail. The DuPont family built this whole empire based on selling these chemicals, and what are we going to do about it? You can't do a damn thing about it, except filter our water and take the fluoride out of it. Anyway, to me that is an analysis. That is the idea that we just keep doing shit, because it is so natural and normal for us not to think beyond the borders of what people say is the right way of thinking, the right stuff to have in your body, the right stuff to have in your mind, and so on.

THE INDIGENOUS WORLDVIEW VERSUS THE WESTERN WORLDVIEW

Each of the five antidotal movements away from Western hegemonic structures shows a movement towards a solution rooted within an Indigenous framework or worldview. I wanted to clarify this worldview discussion as part of the summary of the findings of my study. One way to think about the five antidotal movements to Western hegemony I have uncovered in my study is to imagine that each antidote represents a movement from the Western worldview towards an Indigenous worldview. Hedlund-de Witt (2013) suggests, "Worldviews are then understood as the inescapable, overarching systems of meaning and meaning-making that substantially inform how humans interpret, enact, and co-create reality" (p. 112). According to Ibrahim (1991), our worldview directly affects and mediates our belief systems, assumptions, modes of problem solving, and decision-making (p. 14). A worldview, therefore, defines how one views one's relationship to the outer world, including the environment, other people, and institutions (Sue, 1978).

Tarnas (2006) describes worldviews in a way that is more solid and more concrete:

> Our worldview is not simply the way we look at our world. It reaches inward to constitute our innermost being, and outward to constitute the world. It mirrors but also reinforces and even forges the structures, armorings, and possibilities of our interior life. It deeply configures our psychic and somatic experience, the patterns of our sensing, knowing and interacting with the world. No less potently, our worldview – our beliefs and theories, our maps, our metaphors, our myths, our interpretive assumptions – constellates our outer reality, shaping and working the world's malleable potentials in a thousand ways of subtly reciprocal interaction. World views create worlds. (p. 16)

As a point of clarification, the following chart contrasting the Indigenous worldview and the Western worldview is included to understand the differences, not to suggest that all Indigenous peoples believe the same thing. Nor am I suggesting that all Western people share the same worldview. The reason I am referring to an Indigenous worldview is to understand the differences as they pertain to Western hegemonic influences and the effects of these influences on cultural-level beliefs. There certainly is fluidity based on a variety of factors, such as nature, nurture, culture, family, and so on. An Indigenous person can adopt a Western worldview and orientation, and a Western person can certainly operate from an Indigenous worldview and orientation. These worldviews, and the inherent beliefs of each worldview, are not static; they are dynamic. One of the problems with ayahuasca becoming popular among Western people is the commercialization of ayahuasca in South America, whereby some of the Indigenous people have shifted from a traditional Indigenous worldview towards a Western worldview. At the same time, my impression from conducting qualitative interviews is that some of the interview participants appear to have significantly altered their lives and belief systems to appear to be more akin to an Indigenous worldview, as evidenced through their lifestyles and life choices.

Through my research on Western hegemony, the Western worldview matches up closely with the values and priorities of Western hegemony. At the same time, the Indigenous worldview is therefore grounded within an Indigenous framework, which includes an Indigenous agenda. What follows is a diagram showing the Indigenous worldview versus the Western worldview. The following diagram is primarily based on the research found in Four Arrows and Narvaez (2014) titled, A More Authentic Baseline. Their original diagram and text have been modified to focus on worldviews. In the process of modification, text has been edited and a few distinctions have been added or removed. I have included two other distinctions, one from the work of one of my primary mentors in understanding Indigenous spirituality, Myron Eshowsky (1999), and one from my own observations of the differences in the Western versus Indigenous worldviews.

The Indigenous Worldview versus the Western Worldview

Concept	Western Worldview	Indigenous Worldview
View of Nature	Detachment from, even fear, of nature	Constant awareness and respect for all nonhumans as relatives and teachers
Authentic Social Support	In rhetoric, and for special occasions or crises	A continual high priority
Cultural Mores	Selfishness and stubborness fostered and expected	Generousity and cooperation fostered and expected
Community Involvement	Hierarchical, classist, "us vs." them	Fully egalitarian and cooperative
Socially Purposeful Living	Non-normative self/family/business orientation	Normative
Community Enjoyment	Rare (spectator sports, religious services, events)	Common and authentic
Boundaries	Rigid kinship culture and social classes	Fluid, companion/kinship culture
Social Contact with Others	Minimal. Focused on work, spectator enertainment, superficial interaction	Considerable, including much community contact, such as dancing, singing, playing, ritual
Materialism	Selfishness and accumulation is ultimate	Generosity is ultimate
Conflict Resolution	Goal is usually punishment, revenge or payback	Goal is to bring all back into community
Individual Freedom	Restrictive and subject to authoritarian input, freedom mostly in financial areas and unequal structures	Extensive with no coercion
Individual Relationships	Hierarchical and authoritarian	Egalitarian
Multi-Age Contact	Rare outside of family, avoided otherwise	Continual, sought-after, elders valued
Role Models	Those with high wealth, power, celebrity status	Those with high virtue and commitment to community
Generosity and Cooperation	Selfishness and stubbornness often expected in popular culture	Fostered and expected
Immorality	Cheating, abuse, and deception common and expected	Cheating, abuse, aggression, and deception rare and not tolerated
Fear Orientation	Fear-based and fear avoidance typical	Courage/fearlessness fostered
Ego Emphasis	Concerns of inferiority and superiority are common	Courage/fearlessness fostered Person is "large in life" but never feels superior
Spirituality	A "known" Creator is "exterior" and regarded "occasionally" during stress or on certain days	Mysterious "Creator" is in everything and thus gives sacred significance to all. Ceremony is continual
*Ethical Conduct	Focused on rules, regulations, legal hierarchy	Based on getting along and sustaining relationships
**Experiential Orientation	Virtual experience valued	Direct experience valued and sought after

*Myron Eshowsky (1999) from his essay, *Shamanism and Peace-making*
**Added by Kaufman

Conclusion

This chapter presented the five antidotal movements away from Western hegemony, which were uncovered through my analysis of both my qualitative and quantitative research data. With each antidotal movement, I explained how it was connected to Western hegemony, and then, how the data suggested a unique antidotal movement away from this specific form of Western hegemony. I also explained how the antidotal solution was grounded within an Indigenous perspective. I then included several samples from the qualitative data regarding each antidotal movement to show how the participants reported their changes. When applicable, I also included examples from the quantitative data to show the antidotal movement away from Western hegemony. Specifically, as part of my analysis process, I reconfigured many of the quantitative data charts to show how participants who have worked with ayahuasca more than 50 times reported a different set of data trends than those who have worked with ayahuasca less than 50 times. Oftentimes, participants who have worked with ayahuasca more than 50 times show a significantly larger degree of movement away from hegemonic structures than those who have worked with ayahuasca less than 50 times, and this is evident in many of the data charts. The last part of this chapter showed some of the differences between the Indigenous worldview and the Western worldview. While my research has uncovered some of the ways ayahuasca might be a potential antidote to some hegemonic structures, ayahuasca also poses many challenges, especially in the West. Ayahuasca is not beyond critique. In the next chapter, I explore some of the problems associated with ayahuasca and some of the ways in which, rather than acting to counter Western hegemony, in some cases, it may reinforce hegemony.

CHAPTER 5: Interviews with Experts in the Field of Ayahuasca: Rick Strassman, Alan Shoemaker, and Rak Razam

We often pray to see and experience beauty inside of ourselves and our lives so that we can see beauty outside ourselves and in our every day lives. The ayahuasca sometimes teaches that a person cannot recognize external beauty without seeing inner beauty. So we pray in ceremony for ourselves, our families, and our world to recognize that they are all part of a beautiful world and all a part of beautiful creation.
(Anonymous Ceremony Leader)

INTERVIEW WITH RICK STRASSMAN

This interview took place via email in July 2015. Rick Strassman MD performed the first new human studies with psychedelic drugs in the United States. His research involved the powerful naturally occurring compound, DMT. Strassman's early work led to this substance through his earlier study of the pineal gland as a potential biological locus for spiritual experiences. He administered several hundred doses of DMT to approximately 60 volunteers between 1990 and 1995. He wrote about this research in the popular book, DMT: The Spirit Molecule. Dr. Strassman is currently Clinical Associate Professor of Psychiatry at the University of New Mexico School of Medicine. He is also President and Co-founder of the Cottonwood Research Foundation, which is dedicated to consciousness research.

Do you think ayahuasca can play a role in social change?

Rick Strassman: My sense of how ayahuasca and other psychedelics affect change includes their effects on suggestibility. I do not think that ayahuasca, inherently, is antidotal, but solidifies and strengthens the antidotal beliefs and practices of the specific group or individual. For example, monastic communities all manifest the five movements you articulate above, and ayahuasca plays no role in them. On the other hand, psychedelics can be and have been used for quite nefarious reasons over the centuries, and may just as readily work against the five antidotal movements that you refer to. For example, the Nazi leadership and followers were quite keen on using both psychedelics and Tibetan Buddhism for occult purposes; that is, manipulating spiritual forces for personal gain.

Do you see a connection between working with ayahuasca and combatting Western hegemony?

RS: I think ayahuasca can be enlisted in combating Western hegemony when used in the context. I also think it can be enlisted for the purposes of promulgating Western hegemony if used in that context—for example, stimulating narcissistic and materialistic impulses.

What are your criticisms of ayahuasca usage in the West?

RS: There doesn't seem to be an optimal model by means of which to understand and integrate the psychedelic drug experience, in general, and ayahuasca, in particular. The West is a biblically- oriented culture, focusing on ethical monotheism, which seems absent from any models of the contemporary psychedelic drug effect. Latin American shamanic models, while positing the reality bases of what is apprehended during the state of ayahuasca intoxication, lacks the monotheistic worldview that I believe is necessary for the use of these substances for religious purposes to gain any traction in the larger Western culture.

Do you view hallucinogens as being a potential form of pedagogy?

RS: I see them as increasing one's suggestibility, so to the extent that they are employed in the service of pedagogy, they may increase one's openness to what is being taught.

One of the areas in which ayahuasca and other plant medicines seems to provide is individual-level healing (help with anxiety, PTSD, depression, other sorts of assistance with individual problems), and assistance in creating personal-meaning structures, such as overall purpose and existential-level meaning. I view this as helping individuals find self-determination. Have you noticed personal-level healing happening to people who work with ayahuasca and other plant medicines?

RS: Yes. But, I have also noticed negative and neutral responses to consumption of psychedelics, including ayahuasca.

Does it make a difference to be working within a ceremonial context or within a more institutional setting?

RS: Yes. Set and setting, as well as dose of drug, are the determinants of the psychedelic drug experience. I describe this in great detail in a chapter I wrote for Inner Paths to Outer Space: Journeys to alien worlds through psychedelics and other spiritual technologies (Strassman, Wojtowicz, Luna, & Frecska, 2008) called "Getting ready for the journey."

Do you see this sort of personal-level healing providing inspiration to ultimately look outside of one's self to the outside world to heal or to change?

RS: Not necessarily. It depends on the person and on the ethos of the group. Some neo-Nazi organizations, occultists, very dark hedonists, use psychedelics to increase their commitment to such beliefs and practices. I have met people who use psychedelics to manipulate other people within all manner of contexts: sexually, "power tripping," emotionally, and so on.

What obstacles do you see there being to individuals focusing on larger scale change?

RS: Self-centeredness, passivity, economic and social barriers.

Did you see any changes towards relationality in your work with DMT? If so, what?

RS: Some of our volunteers changed jobs or refocused their current job into areas more consistent with what they perceived during their DMT experiences. But, I wouldn't say this was a change in relatedness. On the other hand, the highly interactive and relational nature of the DMT experience led me to an interactive-relational model for the DMT effect, away from the Buddhist and toward the Hebrew Biblical prophetic, which is a dualistic experience.

I know people who've gotten less related as a result of using DMT. They develop messianic and paranoid worldviews that exclude the outside world. Does this antidotal movement line up to your own view of the role plant teachers play in healing?

RS: No. It's one perspective given the optimal set and setting issues to shape such drug experiences. Even the notion of "plant teachers" seems to presuppose a lot. These are plants that contain chemicals allowing us access to usually invisible forces, processes, and objects. "Teacher" seems biased towards "teaching." These forces can be highly malevolent.

Given that ayahuasca ceremonies are collective experiences and many psychonauts work with hallucinogens solo, how do these two formats reinforce these two ideas (individualism versus relationalty)?

RS: I don't see that as paramount. Solo use can lead to greater or lesser social involvement as can collective use. Of course, when using collectively, one's in a group, but I've been in groups where the individuals resented being in the group.

In my research, there seems to be evidence that over time the ayahuasca experience influences people to move from the belief that only human beings have consciousness and are the only species of importance, towards the view that plants, animals, and the natural world are likewise sentient. For instance, many of the qualitative interview participants reported having reverence for ayahuasca as a living entity, and referring to her as "Grandmother" and as a plant teacher. Have you seen this sort of change in people who worked with DMT (from seeing nature as the only ones having consciousness to viewing plants as having consciousness)?

RS: Since I worked only with pure DMT in a hospital setting, these issues didn't come up. In addition, I did my research in the early 1990s, before ayahuasca had become as popular as it is now. At the same time, some of our volunteers found normally "life-full" things devoid of life, and mechanical, under the influence of DMT, as much as feeling the world to be more full of life than they had sense previously.

Do you agree with this view or disagree with the view that plants and the natural world has consciousness?

RS: It may be that plants have consciousness of a certain sort. One should never underestimate the power of projection, however, upon the non-human world, in thinking it's more like us than perhaps is the case.

Do you think that DMT has consciousness?

RS: No. But I do think DMT can alter our consciousness in unique ways.

Do you see evidence that plant medicines can help people alter their relationship to materialism and consumerism to purpose found beyond these structures?

RS: I don't think it's a function of the plants; but rather, a function of the increased suggestibility to certain notions while under the influence of their pharmacology. Anti-capitalistic notions might be more successfully inculcated, communist/socialist ones, fascist nationalistic ones, too.

Does this assertion (that plant medicines can alter how people relate to consumerism and materialism) seem unfounded to you? If so, why?

RS: It's not the plants; it's how they're used.

Have you seen any shifts in your own priorities regarding materialism and consumerism after researching DMT?

RS: If we enlarge the notion of materialism to include a materialistic basis of reality, of the DMT experience, of the spiritual worlds, then my research has led me to a more spiritual, non-material, perspective. That is, it's convinced me of the reality of the incorporeal worlds and their influence on this one. It also provided an entrée back into ethical monotheism from decades of Buddhist study and practice.

If people who took part in your DMT study suggested that working with DMT was meaningful to them, do you think this type of "meaning" can be extrapolated out to suggest some sort of shift in deep meaning away from materialism and consumerism? How do you think of the deep meaning they found in their DMT experiences?

RS: The primary take-home the research volunteers agreed upon was the existence and nature of the DMT world. Not necessarily any particular meaning associated with it; or rather, no specific informational content beyond what might expected among a group of liberal, secular, educated Westerners living in Albuquerque and Santa Fe.

If hallucinogens "open people up" to other possibilities and other realms of reality, what do you think the implication is in their daily lives of these awarenesses?

RS: Psychedelics can close people down, make them paranoid, not only open them up. How people integrate their experiences is key and most don't have a very good model other than vague Eastern religious or Latin American shamanic models. New Age models partake of those, as well as occultism, psychology. Without a proper model, there's little to be done with the experiences. In fact, with a proper model and without the experiences, more good may ultimately come. But the ideal mix of model and experiences, in my opinion, hasn't been developed and thus a lot of the potential value of the experiences is lost.

What are spiritual experiences? What is spiritual? How can we tell the difference between our own delusions and our own insights? These are questions that are being glossed over in most discussions of the value of the psychedelic drug states.

My research seems to suggest that people become more critical of oppressive structures from their participation in ayahuasca ceremonies. While this antidotal movement away from Western hegemony seems to have the least evidence, I find it an interesting idea to explore. Do you see any such movement in people working with plant medicines towards being more critical?

RS: No. In fact, I find them to be less critical, since much of the organized use of ayahuasca partakes of a cultish atmosphere which discourages criticality; e.g., the sexual and financial abuse of retreatants by group leaders is swept under the rug, as is in the case with any cult with little in the way of peer view and checks and balances.

Do you see evidence of people who work with hallucinogens becoming more apolitical or apathetic after using them?

RS: Psychedelic use in general may be a reaction to a feeling of powerless in the system, which may either be reinforced or discouraged by the set and setting in which the psychedelic experience takes place, and the model with which they integrate their experiences afterwards. It's like the "a-motivational syndrome" that was so popularly discussed in psychiatry as an "effect" of marijuana use in the '70s. Some people prone to apathy get more apathetic, those who need to focus might find marijuana helps them be more productive and active in their pursuits.

Any closing remarks?

RS: Psychedelics are just tools which can be misused, as well as used.

Interview with Alan Shoemaker

Alan Shoemaker is a formally trained ayahuasquero, and writer. He is the author of Ayahuasca Medicine: The shamanic world of Amazonian plant healing. Shoemaker has lectured on curanderismo all over the United States and Europe and has been published in journals including Shaman's Drum, Journal for Peace and Humanities, and Magical Blend. He is the host of the annual International Amazonian Shamanism Conference in Peru, and is the founder of the Soga Del Alma Church (Vine of the Soul). Shoemaker lives outside of Iquitos, Peru, with his two children.

What changes do you see in people who work with ayahuasca?

Alan Shoemaker: Some become more humble, and some don't. Those that don't have misused the medicina to feed their egos. They often begin to call themselves 'shaman', which is never a good sign.

For sure not a good sign. Why do you suppose that is, that some get bigger egos and some become more humble? Isn't the mission of the medicine to have people be more humble and more open to learning?

AS: Absolutely, but many fall prey to what they believe to be some mystical power. In doing so, when they believe it is spirit speaking to them, it isn't, it's their own mind, and their ego. This path isn't for everyone, no matter what you may think. I might love to be a classical pianist, but I just don't have the talent for it, or my fingers are too fat and not long enough, etc. So it is important to realize clearly what is possible and what isn't.

Isn't that one of the inherent problems, since there is no standardization, anyone can call themselves a shaman or a medicine man/woman? This also happens, of course, with people running ceremonies here in the U.S.

AS: Yes, it is a problem, even here in Mecca for ayahuasqueros (Iquitos, Peru). Most are "facilitators" and that's an excellent place to be, but few are actually "shamans."

Do you think that is also the case with the Santo Daime Church, who sometimes work with less strong medicine and conduct their ceremonies in the light?

AS: The Daime have a variety of medicines, depending on the type of ceremony they wish to focus on. Typically, it is rather weak but they can also serve a reduced medicine that is much stronger. When I drank with them in Amsterdam, it was weak and there were some candles lit. They also shared the Light of the Virgin Mary, which is how they refer to the marijuana that is passed around during a gathering.

But it also sounds like you have an idea of what a strong ceremony is like. Can you say more about it? And is there a way to run ceremonies to reduce people's egos versus enhance them, as you started the interview discussing?

AS: A strong ceremony requires a very visual medicina, making no difference if your eyes are closed or open. Typically, seeing spirits moving around, walking thru walls, speaking with you, jaguars, anacondas, etc. A medicine that completely takes you from this mundane world.

When the medicine is this strong, your ego is almost completely shut down. That is the reason ceremonies are held in darkness, so that the light reflecting off surfaces here keeps you focused on this reality.

And you are saying that is rare, even in Peru, where you are? It is certainly rare here in the U.S. where people use candles and do not do ceremonies in the dark, and often make the ceremonies more social, and less intense.

AS: Yes, to get a real quality medicine like I mentioned is quite rare here in Peru. It happens sometimes because the cook got lucky. On the other hand, the big lodges take 30 people every two weeks. Most are not very experienced and so giving them rocket fuel would probably not be that good of an idea. Towards the end of their two-week program, the dose could be increased as they now have more experience with the medicina.

Do you think the medicine has a central message or mission? To me, part of it seems to be expanding the notion of self-determination and enhanced of freedom for people, on all levels.

AS: For most people, the complete understanding/knowledge that there are alternate realities existing alongside ours is sufficient. There are others (people) that, once they have come to this conclusion, work with it and the spirits. That's why there is such a problem with religions. They force a dogma onto you and ask that you just "have faith: in what the "good book" says. Faith is very frustrating.

Dogma certainly is, but don't you think that, if this is a healing path per se, that it's just another Western trap to focus solely on one's own healing without looking outwards to the world, and seeing all the messed up crap out there, and wanting to help. For some, healing themselves is their reason for partaking in ceremony. Beyond that, healing others and making the world a better place to be is the ultimate conclusion, once you have healed yourself, right? Do you think ayahuasca makes a person, over time, more aware of the toxic forces in this world, oppressive dogmas, beliefs, etc?

AS: On any given city block here in Iquitos, there are one or two ayahuasqueros holding their traditional ceremonies on every Tuesday and Friday night, in the back room of their house with the sound of motorcars going by, music coming from the house next door, babies crying, etc. The police told me over 10 years ago that they believed that on any given Friday night, 10% of the population here are drinking ayahuasca, that's 40,000 Peruvians. They go to ceremony not to see visions and hallucinations, although that happens from time to time when the cook got lucky. They drink to purify their body and expel negativity. They understand that there is a lot of negativity in the world and around them and they know that ayahuasca helps. So, in general, ayahuasaca helps to show you what needs to be changed in yourself, about your family, and your environment.

How, then, does it work for Westerners where it is not part of our culture, and people do not regularly participate in ceremony in the US, where even more serious ceremony people often only have access to medicine ceremonies once a month or even less often?

AS: It's the gringos coming that have read many articles published in Shaman's Drum, Magical Blend and other magazines, as well as the published books, that come and want to have the visionary experience they have read about. Unfortunately, that experience does not reside in the bottle of ayahuasca because if it did, I'd have it running with an IV 24-hours a day. It's a gift given from the spirit world when they so desire to.

I think it's obvious that, after seeing such beauty from an aya experience, that you carry that with you which also colors the way you look at the world around you.

AS: Yes!

Do you think it then has people see the contrast; the ugliness, unhealthy people, etc.?

AS: Absolutely! There could be no other conclusion than that.

My research seems to imply that seeing that contrast in experience may inspire people to be more socially and politically critical, including dogmas such as Christianity, and other religious dogmas.

AS: Yeah, for me as well.

Do you think that is common (political activism)? I would think peoople would be really pissed off that the rainforest is being destroyed and corruption runs the world.

AS: Yes, it's common, because it takes someone to be somewhat aware to have come to this path in the first place. Leaving the zombie world behind in search of more light and love.

Interview with Rak Razam, September 2015

Rak Razam is an experiential journalist, writing about and helping shape the emergence of a new cultural paradigm in the 21st century. Author of the book Aya Awakenings: A shamanic odyssey, Razam also wrote, produced and co-directed the documentary Aya: Awakenings. Rak is also the created and host of the podcast series In a Perfect World.

What is the vision you are presenting with ayahuasca and with plant medicines?

Rak Razam: When we think of, what is social change? It brings up, for me, questions of what is a society, what is our culture? And, even if you look at the language of a culture, it's an organism. It is an organism which grows, and is made up in this case of individuals who— Western culture, at least 20th century, 21st century culture, has been very dominated by the idea of the individual. Individuals, in this case, are dominated, to a large degree, by the American dream, or this perception of this capitalist sort of possession of the American dream, into the monetary success story and the taking of resources, and the reinforcement of the ego structure. And, it is very individualstic in the sense that there is this not-so-invisible hierarchy within that. It takes probably tens of thousands, if not more people, in a hierarchical structure for that person at the top to be the CEO-millionaire-person who has the power and the ability to wield or to manifest that capitalist wet dream. For me, that's what comes to mind when we think of culture.

When we think of medicine plants and things like ayahuasca and entheogens in general, I come back to some of the most pronounced properties, and there's quite a few really, in the sense of the ego dissolving or full- spectrum-consciousness revealing, in the sense that it's not about just this drive of the ego to consume and reinforce and protect and conquer, and that's dominated culture, as Terrence McKenna used to call it. It is something for me, having now had almost a decade of experience myself with plant medicines, dogmatic culture feels so wrong. It feels like it is a sickness. It feels like it is something that is reinforcing one aspect of the human organism at the detriment of the whole organism, and also of the whole culture of organisms that make up the human race. The human race as well is just one strand of species within a collective whole, within the Gaian matrix. So there's this dichotomy between, I guess, dominated culture and the ego and what we think of as culture and what the plant medicines reveal

So, when the ego is dissolving—I find in ayahuasca, one of the sort of initiatory-phase responses is this—can be this mental sorting and emotional body information comes up from the unconscious. The unconscious comes up into the conscious mind, and any traumas or hidden issues or things you've buried in your psyche come up into the conscious mind to be dealt with, and to be released and resorted and defragged, and in that sorting a full spectrum of information comes up. That's one layer of the process of releasing the grip of the individual ego. And, in the next layer, quite often I'll have this dissolution or merging back into the web of life and what's around me energetically.

With the sensory input, with the sounds of the jungle and nature, there can be this complete merging back into the web of life. So all the signals my brain is receiving, and that's not just on a mental level, but on a very heart-based level of feeling, this very intricate web of life, and the signals that nature is giving off, and the animals and the wind and the storm. And, sometimes there's this very Gestalt-type feeling that I'm not just part of all that, but I can reach out energetically and influence all that, just as nature is influencing me. So there's this reabsorption back into a larger collective of consciousness, which is nature's consciousness, and that is a culture, as well.

So this idea of culture for me is like, what is culture? Even when you look within subcultures, you can see ayahuasca cultures or medicine cultures or Indigenous cultures—they are all subsections. Perhaps in those examples, they all relate to medicine and relating to medicine as it brings them back to the earth and to the planet and into the planetary matrix, and on into the web of life as far as it goes. But, I'm coming to some interesting sort of intuitions and feelings around what we make as a collective when we are on that frequency, when we are tuned in, and even when we're not tuned in, we're still all connected. But when we are aware of the frequency of that connection through a rise in consciousness, it doesn't have to be medicine-mediated. It could be through meditation, it could be through technology with a lot of the neuroscience and EEG technologies and biofeedback, etc.

That's on one level, but I don't think you can say that's a consistent experience, what you are talking about that's the potential of the plant to open up to this universe of interconnectedness and healing. But that's not the case for a lot of people, too. One of the threads of my research is people who work with plant medicines consistently in somewhat of a disciplined way, the result of what you're talking about, the opening, is there. But other people who just do this recreationally or as a one-off experience, don't necessarily have that. It might just be a hell night, or it might just be boring, it may just be any number of experiences.

RR: I agree, but the thing is still present and there in potential in situ ready for the seeker who wants to go deeper. It's the same with other modalities, like sex, you might not achieve the optimal tantric perfection your first go. But if you continue on the path of recognizing energy and recognizing how to work with this energy, you will end up on these very pronounced interior landscapes of the mind, heart, and soul.

So, I think things with ayahuasca, I would say we are sort of in the third wave of ayahuasca usage in the West at the moment. As the first hundred or so years, Richard Spruce, the first botanical expeditions all the way through to about 1990, one of the first Western lodges, Sachamama in Iquitos, the first wave of ayahuasca tourism, and still the early adopters and the seekers. It really has not solidified down to this now sort of lifestyle choice, ayahuasca, sort of cultural uptake where people know about its medicinal qualities and its healing potentials. So, we are in this sort of third wave post-Shimbre, post-that very public ayahuasca death at the center in Puerto Maldonado.

Ayahuasca has become a global brand now. And it has become a global brand in Western culture across the world, and it is known for its medicinaland healing qualities. People are still on the first wave of the psychic journey with it. The reason why it is spreading so rapidly and is so popular and successful—the chief amongst them is that it works, and it helps people come to face their demons and face their health issues and, in some instances, get control of their health and their selves. But for me, that's just the first leg of the journey. We all need to be cleansed of the things which are blocking our full potential, and then when you go deeper, once you are cleansed, and the organism of the human body and the bioelectric field, and your ability to connect to the higher dimensions, that's the next level. And, it transcends the commodification of ayahuasca within the Western culture. Potentially, it opens up the shamanic paradigm or the perception of the shamanic paradigm, within which I mean a living organism and a living universe, back to the archaic sense of Pachamama, and the Indigenous understanding of the world is this living being that we are embedded in, and we need to seek right relationship with. So, I really think this wave of ayahuasca usage we are going through globally at the moment is because so many people are sick from the toxification of Western culture and people need a medicine. So, at the apex of this sickness, ayahuasca is resurging back into our culture to help rebalance us.

It doesn't mean necessarily—not everyone has to stay on the ayahuasca path, but it doesn't mean necessarily that the work is over once the ceremony is over, whether you've done one ceremony or a hundred or a thousand. It means the more you plug into what's really going on here on planet Earth, it transforms you, and then through you, one by one, and transforms the culture. It is not just ayahuasca that's doing that, I believe it's the planetary organism, it's the intelligence of nature, which is alive and well, and is shaping us for the desired result, the optimal result.

I totally hear you. A couple things that you're saying underline what I've been finding about Western hegemony. One of them is the Western belief, of course, that humankind is dominant over the earth, and animals and plants are under the subjugation of human beings. And, when people work with medicine, there's a complete shift in their relationship with earth and with nature. And, through ayahuasca, you can't help but think that maybe there is some consciousness to this plant, because it's so intense and has so many variables and so many flavors of the medicine.

But, at least for me, I think part of the—you used the phrase, "you see what's really going on." I think that comes down to criticality, that's where I—not necessarily in the political sense, but you see the fabric and the workings of the psyche to the point where you are able to be more critical of—not only commodification, but greed, and on some social level, to look at politics differently. A person would then, by extension, look at corruption differently, because it seems completely in contrast to the ways of medicine. That's kind of hard for me to get my hands around in some kind of scientific sense, or even measurably. However, it just seems to be that way—that people who work with medicine have a different relationship to criticality, in general.

RR: I think it is important you use that word criticality. It is important not to get too daft and woo-woo about things. But what we're really saying here is we're bridging paradigms. There are two different paradigms, and they speak different languages. It is like two different parts of the brain, they both might be valid, but you are just looking at them from different perspectives.

It is like that quote from Albert Einstein, I can't remember the exact words, something like the level of consciousness which sort of causes the problem isn't going to be the level of consciousness which fixes the problem and gets you out of it. It seems to me that as well as this criticality of looking at all the ills and problems of our culture. I mean, ayahuasca can also be an amazing tool for looking at the human mind itself.

I feel, again, that the process is about getting to know your mind, and getting to know which bits of the ego, and what happens when this energetic pulse sort of drops in and you get all this energy and different aspects of the mind, and the brain start to riff off and go in different directions. But, that criticality can also be applied in ayahuasca sense to knowing yourself, and knowing the brain, and knowing the ego. And, I think that, talking about different paradigms, there is a growing movement, actually. There are so many different strands of ayahuasca culture now that I'm seeing developing. It's just mutating so rapidly. Basically, I guess it would be interesting to see someone do a dissertation or a comment on the different modalities that have come from the East, like meditation, and yoga, and martial arts, and Tantra, and now ayahuasca, not coming from the East, but from Indigenous cultures, because the vectors and the disseminations, sort of streams, seem to be following very similar patterns, where Western culture takes them on board, and sort through what they think the dogmas are, and they take bits they want, and tweak it and build their own takes on it, which is a natural way of growth and integration into western culture.

But there are things now like "aya-yoga," which is retreats doing a heavy focus on yoga and ayahuasca, and I think that works really well. These modalities complement very well, as do things like meditation. And, I've even seen—there's a lot of interest in neuroscience, wiring people up with EG helmets now, and trying to look at what's happening in the brain when people are on ayahuasca.

You should come to my town, that's where a lot of the brain research is happening with Richie Davidson at the Center for Investigating Healthy Minds.

RR: Yeah, I am really getting into neuroscience. I'm working with a few different people, looking at different aspects and documenting and making maps. I am also looking at entrainment with tryptamines in general, through different modalities of tryptamines where they're legal. It's an enormous growth opportunity for phrenology, and we seem to have tangibly tools to look at that criticality. And this is the thing, it's like all right, we are in a subjective experience. We are seeing a vision of Madre Ayahuasca, or the planet, or a snake or whatever, and we are an emotional experience and we are having these amazing thoughts. It's all subjective. And, neuroscience actually says none of its subjective; it's all some sort of objective brain neuron firing. Technically, maybe they can measure what's happening in what area of the brain, maybe they can see the electrical impulses. But they don't know you've just contacted your dead mother and she's forgiven you for that time something that happened when you were 12. It's these two worlds, and it seems they are being breached.

Basically, what I have come to realize is these substances are catalysts to reveal what we have within us already. The plants are just mediators and teachers for us to remember what we can already do as humans and all these previous cultures have the maps of consciousness to show us and to remember us. They are boot-strapping up and they are making it happen faster because it seems there's a bit of urgency on the planet at the moment. But, it's like we are the actual operating system. We are the operating system to ourselves.

I agree, that's what's so good about meditation with ayahuasca that it giving you a grounding in your body and in your own direct experience without it becoming kooky and weird. The only problem, and that's not the right word—I've sat with so many different groups in the United States where that isn't the case, where there isn't applied learning. Where there's sort of "the dark side of the light chaser" kind of thing happening, without any of the depth, and there's a lot of pushing off of the shadow and pushing off the heaviness of the jungle medicine or whatever. Has that been your experience? Because what you're describing seems more like a panacea or romanticizing ayahuasca.

RR: The whole thing is to look at the context. As I said, we are in this third wave of Western ayahuasca integration. The first wave was, like, 150 years, the second wave was, like, 20-21 years. Now everything is getting faster and faster. The waves of mutation as it comes in the culture is speeding up. If you look at the whole thing as a process, and not just this happening and this is not good and this is good. It's all a process, so most people have got the healing, and once they've got the healing, there's different levels of teaching and engagement. And there's also this mutated different styles of western modalities of entheogens and ayahuasca. There's things like Daime, which is really great for many people, they like that structure. They are doing a very specific thing with their practice. They are making a Gestalt organism and they are praying and charging up the astral, fighting demons and bringing light. They are not doing healing per se, like on an individual level.

So the Peruvian style, which is probably the most predominant ayahuasca from an Indigenous perspective, even within that, perhaps the Shipibo style, that was originally really focused on healing. And, it came from a lineage where the curandero or shaman originally was the one who drank, and not the patient. And, it was for the ailments of the local Indigenous people, which were often very physical-based and stomach gastro-type things, and there's bugs that would get in the Amazon, and the ayahuasca would be a physical ailment for that. Or, there was sorcery involved, and the curandero would be sorting out sorcery or bad energy that had been projected around.

But, then as that's coming to the Western style, the Westerners are seeking visions. What I was first told when I went to the Amazon to research my book, which became the film Aya: Awakenings, many years ago now, was that many westerners coming down to seek the wisdom of the curanderos. They didn't have a physical sickness. Many people do, and they make the headlines about the healing modalities of ayahuasca, but the vast majority were coming down and seeking visions. The vision seekers—the famous Kyra Salak article, which was in National Geographic in 2006 pointed out, called it "Vision Seekers." And, it sort of related to this whole '60s-generation, psychedelic-psychonaut generation in the West is that we need to see, we needed to see something in a vision to believe it was real. Even within a psychedelic culture, where it's all subjective, and there's not that criticality perhaps of the culture or other paradigms, but even in their culture, they needed to see something to believe in it in that way.

That changed the whole dynamic, and then a lot of those streams are still very alive and healthy and well at the moment. Ayahuasca tourism is happening all through Peru and other South American countries. But, there's that stream. And, then a lot of the people that have been working with the medicine from the second wave have come back to their homes throughout the world and have continued to work with the medicine. There's been a generation of neo-shamanic facilitators rise up, and some of them have retained the Peruvian style. Many don't have the training, they don't have that expertise of decades of experience with plant medicines and the wide spectrum of healing that a curandero would do with not just ayahuasca.

It goes beyond just healing. You have people who have gone back to the West and are practicing. Many people in the West have never been to South America. They have only learned from other Westerners who have been the seeders and the bridges between the two cultures, and there has been a dilution of a dilution of how it's done. This is a natural transference of a meme and the way it evolves, and it's all good.

I think we are going to see, even with those people who have stayed on the medicine path, we have rejected what they see as the dogma of the Indigenous approach, if they stay on it and they work with it, the medicine will teach, and it will reboot a depth of quality of interaction and of knowledge. And, I think we are going to see a generation of Western shamans blossoming over the next few years. We have been and we are seeing that.

But what we're seeing—and I've talked to many different ayahuasca commentators about this—what we're seeing—one of my podcasts with Dennis McKenna—I think we called it "Globalhuasca" talks about this whole idea, that basically we are in the third wave of western ayahuasca usage. And, somewhere towards the maturity of this wave, I think what we will be seeing is not just the establishment of not just the lodge system, which is established at the moment, but more like a monastery system, more like a thing where those people who have been on the path for quite awhile go, "I can't just keep going back recreationally, I need a longer immersion in the knowledge and in the plant world." And, if you can't do that in Peru, we are going to see that in the west. You are going to see systems of support spring up which are for long-term plant medicine Jedis who are training, really.

This is what I'm getting at, is that basically, then that level of just going for healing or just going for whatever they are at now, it's a process, and where it's a long game. It's playing a long game, and this is how it transfers the knowledge of plant medicines and not just ayahuasca, but what ayahuasca is spearheading which is a planetary resurgence and reintegration of plant medicines which connect to the planetary intelligence, and plug us back into right relationship, hopefully.

But that learning and that knowledge transfer is different. I have spoken to people, however, who have taken crash courses in ayahuasca shamanism and come back acting like they are experts. It seems like there is an arrogance about it and a danger, because they are bringing people into ceremony and they are doing heavy, dark shit with no sensitivity to how it's being received and no experience with working with people in that vulnerable state. I think what you are saying is true, it's a work in progress—but I don't know if you see what I see, if you have these experiences of meeting people, the arrogance and sort of the danger that they pose in the ceremony world. People quit their jobs and, again, I'm critical of the commodification and the materialism, and people who quickly claim, "I'm gonna move to Peru and become a famous shaman." They have one vision and they think they are God's gift to everything, and there's a lot of danger.

RR: Any modality that has survived the test of time—like a spiritual modality, body modality or martial arts or meditation or yoga—it's because they transmit and accuracy of this is how it must be done and you're not meant to deviate from it. And different modalities mutate and they can improve upon or extend, but there's a core set of rules that have been created for a reason, and then it's the integrity of that transmission that allows it to actually survive. If it becomes dissolute and weakened and watered down for the reason to pander to consumerism or whatever, then it's not really satisfying, usually, its core reason for being. I would think that that's part of the structure. If you look at memes and genes, if you look at the thing which is being transmitted, the structure of itself has integrity as it replicates from one generation to the next. I would hazard a guess that a lot of spiritual modalities and the things you have to do are to instill focus and to instill a rigor of discipline which is needed for the adept. And, that discipline is largely lacking from Western society across the board.

Many new people are coming—the entry point for them and their level of consciousness or what their expectations are. Ayahuasca is getting a lot of press—it was in the New York Times like six months ago, or something, in the Lifestyle section. It is a fad thing for a lot of the cool sort of frequency, or the consciousness festival, Burning Man, LA crowd. There is an expectation around that, again, which is not what the medicine is. You take this thing—it's the newest thing. You take this thing and it does this.

As we know, with ayahuasca, you take that thing, and it freaking opens you up. It challenges you and it says, now you have got to do this work with me. It's about you doing the thing, not ayahuasca just doing it for you. It is engaging you in a process of healing and discovery. It is taking you to the mat. Just like the teacher would do with you on the outside.

As a teacher plant, and this is what they would call them in Indigenous cultures. These are the teacher plants. And, teachers sometimes have to be hard on the students. And, I think for the commodified level of ayahuasca in the culture that is wanting it just as the latest thing, they just don't understand that level of what it is, of the teacher plant. They think of it like, it is a drink, you take it, and it does this. But, they are not tuning in yet to this thing that you are going to get your ass kicked. You've got to do hard work. It can be the hardest work ever. And, it's asking you to do that. And, if you don't do that, you just go around in loops and loops and loops until you are ready to do the work. So, there are different levels of expectation that need to be looked at, as well.

CHAPTER 6: Problems with Ayahuasca Usage in the West and by Westerners

See the light in your eyes
In your eyes, see the light
Even in the darkest moments of the night
Even in the darkest moments of your life
See the light shining in your heart
In your heart, see the light
Even in the sweetest moments of the night
Even in the sweetest moments of your life.
(Ayahuasca healing song, used by permission
from Anonymous Ceremony Leader)

It would be irresponsible of me to not include an exploration of some of the problems with ayahuasca usage and the peoples who work with ayahuasca, both in South America and in the West. As a researcher, it would be unrealistic to present a one-sided view of ayahuasca as being only of benefit without exploring some of the major challenges it presents. Many of the problems related to ayahuasca were uncovered during my qualitative research interiews, in particular, with the ayahuasca Ceremony Leader. Furthermore, I discovered other problems with ayahuasca usage in my literature research on ayahuasca. Ayahuasca is clearly not a panacea, nor always a clear path towards remedying hegemony. This chapter explores some of the ways in which working with ayahuasca in the West, rather than being an antidote to Western hegemony, appears to be a byproduct of Western hegemony and in support of hegemonic structures and Eurocentric views and beliefs. This chapter explores some of the manifestations of hegemony in the form of commodification such as, cultural appropriation, abuse of power by ayahuasca ceremony leaders, drug tourism, the influence of Christianity on ayahuasca legality, and a critique of psychonauts.

Contextually, many of the challenges related to ayahuasca as an antidote to Western hegemony stem from the tendency of Western users of ayahuasca to view and experience ayahuasca within a Western paradigm or worldview, and not within an Indigenous context or worldview. In the process, the ayahuasca experience, which, at its root, is an Indigenous ceremonial experience, loses its context in translation. This disruption in context oftentimes comes down to a difference in values between the two worldviews.

Ayahuasca Cannot Be Understood

The current rise in ayahuasca usage among Westerners is a relatively new phenomenon. As a result, it is unclear what the long-term results or the effects of Westernization on the ayahuasca experience or the Western psyche will be. The forces of Western hegemony tend to push towards the standardization of its models of medicine, health, healing, and education. Hall (1992) argues that Western research models focus on categorization, condensing complex systems into a system of representation, producing standard models and averages for the purpose of comparison, and creating criteria to evaluate against and rank. Very little about ayahuasca and the ayahuasca experience involves standardization. The brew, for example is never made exactly the same every time. The quantity of DMT is never the same. Each batch is slightly different. Furthermore, some of the people who make ayahuasca include different plants to customize the brew based on the needs of the people drinking it. This lack of standardization suggests that applying a Western scientific approach to attempt to understand ayahuasca may be challenging or useless.

The Western academic approach to examining ayahuasca usage is the push towards codification, for example. With the focus on codification comes arrogance in trying to understand and codify such a mysterious and unknown process as the ayahuasca experience. While some academic researchers are looking at the medical properties and uses of DMT, a detailed history of ayahuasca does not appear to exist in academia. It is possible that many groups use ayahuasca in secret and do not want their knowledge shared with outsiders. Some of the ancient uses of peyote, for instance, exist, but very little exists on how ayahuasca was used hundreds and thousands of years ago. The Western mind, as discussed earlier, has a difficult time accepting that some things are mysterious and may remain mysteries. The Western orientation puts limitations around direct experiences by having to constantly try to understand them, versus the Indigenous model that allows experience to be limitless and unfold in their own time. We do not know why ayahuasca ceremonies take place late at night, for example, and often in the dark; the entire ayahuasca process is mysterious. Indigenous peoples at least have a cosmological understanding that it is okay for things to simply be mysterious and to not be understood, that they can remain a mystery. The Western orientation to "figure out" versus "experience" applies here, and suggests this split in consciousness. The history of ayahuasca usage is also unclear. As Beyer (2012) asserts, "The first ethnobotanical account of ayahuasca dates from 1851, although not published until 1873, when the English botanist Richard Spruce encountered the vine among the Tukano of the Rio Uapes in Brazil." This detail supports the notion that we in the West only recently have even heard about ayahuasca usage, let alone understand how it was originally used, or the ways in which ancient ceremonies were conducted. In fact, most ayahuasca history and chronologies are simply speculative. We have minimal idea of how it was discovered, how it was originally used, and what we do know is speculative at best.

Another enigma of ayahuasca is the mystery surrounding the ways traditional ayahuasca healers have worked, and still work, with ayahuasca. Proctor (2001) explains that, in some ayahuasca traditions, only the ayahuasca leader consumed the ayahuasca, not the patient. The ayahuasca shaman would consume ayahuasca as part of the process to diagnose and cure illness (p. 15). The Peruvian ayahuasca healing center, Temple of the Way of Light (2015), echos the comments made by Proctor; "Traditionally, in the Amazon (although not in all Indigenous tribes), the patient would not drink ayahuasca. Only the curandero would, in order to cleanse the energetic issues of the patient, as well as receive a diagnosis and prescription from doctor ayahuasca." We do not know how long ayahuasca healers have allowed others to drink ayahuasca. There is very little history documented, outside of a few people's travel logs to South America.

Lack of Standardization

There is also very little standardization in the format and setting of ayahuasca ceremonies, in Peru as well as in the West. Some groups function in a more Indigenous fashion than others. Some groups in the West, for instance, play prerecorded music on an iPod, and everyone lays down and has their own ayahuasca experience, which supports a self-centered, individualistic experience representative of the Western worldview. Some groups, inspired by the Church of Santo Daime, require participants to wear white clothes, separate the men and women, distribute song books, play music, and ecourage everyone to sing along. Some of the songs are in English and others in Portuguese, following the Brazilian Daime Church tradition. Other groups conduct ayahuasca ceremonies more like they do in rural Peru, where the ayahuasca healer sings icaros (ancient ayahuasca songs), uses tobacco as a healing technique, and the ceremony is conducted primarily in the dark. There are certainly other groups in places such as Brazil and Colombia who come from their own Indigenous traditions and conduct their ceremonies within their own traditional context, with minimal influence from the West and Western ways of working with ayahuasca. There is a huge variety of settings in which ayahuasca is consumed in the West, as well. Some yoga centers illegally sponsor ayahuasca ceremonies, as do some intentional communities, along with a large group of people interested in American Indian spirituality. There is simply no standard; there is a spectrum of different ayahuasca ceremony styles, from more Indigenous-based ceremonies to Western-oriented ceremonies. There is no standardization in the formats and styles of ceremonies, including group size, which makes it challenging to research and come up with a baseline for style or experience. Embracing these differences, we can certainly gauge if a particular group or ceremony leader is relating to ayahuasca as a sacred plant teacher, simply a drug to trip on, or a Christianized ritual.

Furthermore, there is a lack of standardization of skill level and competence in those leading ayahuasca ceremonies. Within an Indigenous model of scholarship, a person might apprentice with a leader and knowledge and experience will happen through direct teachings from the mentor and indirectly through ceremonial experiences over time. The mentor guides the student in his/her own unique learning process, which includes finding one's own skill set and own knowledge base through dialogue. A mentor then empowers the student to find his/her own way over time as s/he moves towards competence. The Western model of scholarship, in contrast, is primarily based on what Freire (2004) refers to as the "banking system" of education whereby a teacher "deposits" information into a passive student's mind for the student to know long enough to regurgitate during testing.

CULTURAL APPROPRIATION

Some of the ways in which ayahuasca ceremonies in the West are influenced by Western hegemony is connected to cultural appropriation. Many Western people are now leading and participating in ayahuasca ceremonies without respect for the cultural context and significance in which ayahuasca is situated within Indigenous cultures. Western participants in ayahuasca ceremonies oftentimes appear to have lack of understanding of the customs, legality, history, and sacrifices made by Indigenous experts working with ayahuasca.

According to Rogers (2006), cultural appropriation can be defined as the use of, "a culture's symbols, artifacts, genres, rituals" (p. 474). Rogers identifies four categories of cultural appropriation:

1. Cultural exchange: the reciprocal exchange of symbols, artifacts, rituals, genres, and/or technologies between cultures with roughly equal levels of power.

2. Cultural dominance: the use of elements of dominant culture by members of a subordinated culture in a context in which the dominant culture has been imposed onto the subordinated culture...

3. Cultural exploitation: the appropriation of elements of a subordinated culture by a dominant culture without substantial reciprocity, permission, and/or compensation.

4. Transculturation: cultural elements created from and/or by multiple cultures, such that identification of a single originating culture is problematic. (p. 477)

For many people who live in areas where ayahuasca ceremonies have been conducted for thousands of years, ayahuasca and its cultural and spiritual significance play a part in every day life. Tupper (2009a) explained, "For many indigenous peoples of the Amazon, ayahuasca is integral to ritual practices, myths, cosmologies, art and music, and most other aspects of cultural life" (p. 118). I appreciate Rogers' explanation of cultural appropriation, and his inclusion that one aspect of cultural appropriation is the way in which the dominant culture uses elements of a subordinated culture out of context and without permission. In this case, Western people often misuse and misrepresent themselves as being connected to certain Indigenous ayahuasca groups when they are not.

Referencing Western versus Indigenous worldview concepts, it appears that Western users of ayahuasca may have unintentionally applied a Western worldview to working with this Indigenous plant teacher. This is the very nature of Western hegemony that it is something perpetuated unconsciously by the masses. According to Mezey (2007), "To think of culture more dynamically requires asking about power, appropriation, and negotiations between groups" (p. 2006). From this lens, power and appropriation point to Westerners using economic power to exploit ayahuasca culture, and oftentimes Indigenous peoples, who traditionally work with this plant teacher. The ayahuasca ceremonies and the structures of the ceremonies are certainly a form of cultural property (music, art, healing techniques, and ceremony structures). The ayahuasca ceremony is how some ayahuasca cultures, such as the Shipibo in Peru, self-identify. When one culture borrows or adapts another culture's property, such as the ayahuasca ceremonies, they, in essence, create a watered-down version of the real thing, based on very limited exposure, limited experiences, and stereotypes of Indigenous peoples and healers. Western people using ayahuasca have economic power and the ability to commodify the ayahuasca experience, and, within Western hegemony, this is what tends to happen. Commodification of ayahuasca will be examined in depth in the next section.

The same dynamic of Westerners culturally appropriating of Indigenous spiritual practices happened to the American Indians. Deloria (1992), discussing New Agers who have taken parts of American Indian spirituality argued, "They [New Agers] take from the tribal traditions those things they find most attractive, ignoring the cultural context in which those elements were formed and from which they derive their meaning and power" (p. 19). The Western New Age Movement is often accused of commodifying Indigenous spiritual practices and traditions and instead tends to look only at the mystical and mythological aspects of Indigenous spiritual traditions, without understanding or looking at the larger picture of the lives of Indigenous peoples, which oftentimes includes oppression and colonization by Western forces. Part of Western hegemonic structures is the tendency to commodify alternative forms of spirituality and mysticism and turn them into something that can be bought and sold, even if that is not how those traditions work (Rogers, 2006, p. 488). The tendency of the Western New Age Movement, which is similar to the way many Westerners relate to ayahuasca, is that they ignore the forces of Western hegemony that have harmed these Indigenous cultures, and do very little to contribute to Indigenous communities and peoples. Instead, many Westerners operate from a place of individuality and pursue their own agenda without concern for relationality.

Lack of Attribution. Furthermore, Westerners often take pieces of other cultures without providing attribution. Since Judeo-Christian traditions are often culturally familiar and prevalent to Westerners, while ayahuasca traditions are less understood and prevalent, some Westerners essentially come to the conclusion that ayahuasca culture is "up for grabs" and can be used any way they want. This means using ayahuasca songs, art, ceremony structures, and cosmologies out of context and/or without permission, or selling aspects of Indigenous ayahuasca ceremonies and culture to other Westerners. Western hegemonic structures promote consumer culture. Consumer culture views everything as a commodity; including lifestyle, tradition, identity, and even spirituality. Everything in consumer culture is for sale, including spirituality and ceremonies (Aldred, 2000).

In a Western religious context, it would be inappropriate to represent one's self as something one is not. A person cannot call himself or herself a rabbi or a priest, yet people call themselves a medicine man, an ayahuasca expert, a shaman, an elder, or other spiritual titles without repercussion or outrage (Khadem, 2008, p. 203). However, some Westerners are now selling ayahuasca services to other Westerners, and have taken the power away from Indigenous people to dictate what is considered real and what is not considered real, in terms of ayahuasca healing techniques and ceremonies, including which elements of ayahuasca ceremonies should be shared publicly and which should be kept secret. When the dominant culture suddenly dictates which aspects of the non-dominant culture are real and not real, everyone suffers. There has been a tendency for White shamanic practitioners, whom some American Indians refer to as "plastic medicine men," to misrepresent themselves as being part of a particular Indigenous lineage when they are not. These Western people often profit from Indigenous cultural and spiritual rituals and ceremonies such as sweat lodges, ceremonies, vision quests, seminars, and healings, without sharing the financial profit with Indigenous people, and oftentimes not even offering attribution to the cultures these rituals and ceremonies come from (Aldred, 2000; Tupper, 2002). Many South American people are now claiming to be ayahuasca healers and experts to simply cash in on the demand, but do not have the proper training. Furthermore, many Westerners are also claiming to be trained as ayahuasca ceremony leaders without having the proper training over time, or the blessings of their elders/mentors in their work with ayahuasca. Many Westerners are also cashing in on the ayahuasca phenomenon and leading ayahuasca ceremonies in countries, such as the United States.

Romanticizing Indigenous Peoples

Another form of cultural appropriation is Westerners' frequent romanticization of Indigenous cultures and healers, including ayahuasca healers. These same sorts of misconceived mythologies have occurred in Westerners' perception of South American ayahuasca leaders and cultures practicing ayahuasca spirituality. Romanticizing, and, therefore, trivializing, Indigenous practices supports the Western worldview, as does exalting Indigenous practices. The result of romanticizing Indigenous cultures is the tendency to reinforce the "noble" and "ignoble" savage myths of these peoples. These two myths romanticize and demonize the roles of Indigenous peoples, and minimize the seriousness and uniqueness of their histories. The abuses against American Indians have been more extensively documented than those against most other Indigenous groups; however, this tendency to portray American Indian people as noble and ignoble savages also happens within ayahuasca cultures in South America, and in how ayahuasca leaders in particular are depicted. Within American Indian culture, the noble savage is represented by imagery of American Indians in headdresses, and includes the Dances with Wolves and Pocahontas stories. Another popularized noble savage image is the "one-with-the-earth" motif (Mihesuah, 1996). The 1970s "Keep it Beautiful" campaign, featuring Iron Eyes Cody shedding a single tear in response to pollution, reinforced stereotypes about American Indians as closer to nature, stoic, heroic, and noble. These depictions of American Indians are archetypal caricatures created by anthropologists and ethnographers through art and literature. In essence, these images depict a caricature of a culture, mythologized versions of a culture seen through the eyes of Eurocentric romanticism (Bataille, 2001). Eurocentric hegemonic influences extend power to dictate cultural stories, histories, and can manufacture images of Indigenous peoples the way they want, because they have the power to do so.

Within ayahuasca cultures, the same is also true in the depiction of healers and ayahuasqueros. Many Westerners who work with ayahuasca romanticize the lives of ayahuasca healers. Websites advertising ayahuasca retreats in Peru, for example, feature pictures of ayahuasca healers wearing traditional tribal clothing, preparing ayahuasca in the jungle over a large open fire, or smoking a ceremonial pipe, sitting in a traditional maloca, the traditional round ceremonial building where ayahuasca ceremonies are held. While these images of ayahuasca leaders may be accurate insofar as conducting ayahuasca ceremonies, they do not depict a realistic image of these people's lives or their actual lifestyle, which is grounded in the mundane, just as it is in the spiritual. Instead, these advertisement-driven images reinforce stereotypes without presenting a whole view of these healers, their lives, and the cultures from which they come.

The Influence of Christian Hegemony on Legality and Illegality

One of the key reasons Westerners travel to South America to drink ayahuasca and participate in ayahuasca ceremonies is due to the illegality of ayahuasca in the West. As mentioned in Chapter 1, in the United States, ayahuasca is considered a Schedule One drug. Legality is significant in the discussion about challenges with ayahuasca, because who determines legality, and which Indigenous practices should or should not be legislated by the government, is a direct correlate to Western hegemonic structures in the form of legality. Why do many Western governmental bodies frame the work with plant medicines, such as ayahuasca and peyote, as drugs and, therefore, illegal, except if they are done within a Christianized context? By Christianized, I am referring to the legal status of the Christian-based Santo Daime Church in Oregon and the Uniao do Vegetal Church in New Mexico being granted legal rights to work with ayahuasca under the religious freedom law. Why is it that only a Christian-based group can use ayahuasca legally, while Indigenous groups are not afforded the same legal protection? As Kivel (2013) argues, Christian values dominate all aspects of U.S. society; nothing is unaffected (p. 3). Christian hegemony has historically been, and continues to be, a destructive force against anything it deems to be in conflict with its beliefs. Christianity has been a historic force against American Indians. According to Churchill (2002), between 1880 and 1930, 80% of all American Indian children were sent to Christian missionaries, forced to live in Christian-based boarding schools, forbidden from practicing their Indigenous religions and from speaking their native languages (p. 57).

The influence of Christian hegemony was part of the push to outlaw many American Indian spiritual practices, including working with peyote. Peyote in the United States was made illegal in the 1880s. Around 1915, American Indian groups formed the Native American Church to regain legal status to conduct peyote ceremonies. From 1916-1919, Christian groups in the United States spearheaded an anti-peyote lobbying campaign and succeeded in keeping peyote illegal. Maroukis (2012) explains that there appears to be significant evidence that Christian elements were added to this Indigenous-based ceremony (peyote) to acquire legal protection and lessen the opposition against it (pp. 124-126). This shows that the only way American Indians thought they could regain their legal rights to work with peyote was to placate the Christian hegemons who were in power.

It wasn't until the American Indian Religious Freedom Act of 1978 that most religious rights of American Indians were restored. The act gave American Indians the right to have access to sacred sites, to possess eagle feathers and certain bones, as well as use of peyote in sacred ceremonies. Even today, many chapters of the Native American Church still incorporate elements of Christianity into its peyote ceremonies and rituals. In some Native American Church chapters, they sing Christian songs as part of the peyote ceremonies and may even include Bible quotations. Yet Maroukis (2012) argues, "The Native American Church is not indigenized Christianity. It is an indigenous faith, and so perceived by its members, in spite of Christian accreditations to its ceremonies" (p. 69).

Christian hegemony is still an influence on Western society today, and is part of how the American judicial system legislates around what constitutes a legal sacrament, such as ayahuasca or peyote; what constitutes a religion, such as whether or not American Indians can practice their Indigenous forms of spiritualty; and what constitutes morality and ethics. In the case of ayahuasca, Christianity still plays a significant role in determining if groups can legally work with or use ayahuasca or not and under what guidelines. Within the current paradigm, if the groups want legislative support, the ceremonies must be done in a Christian-inspired manner or they will not be legally recognized. Conducting ayahuasca ceremonies in an Indigenous framework is not enough to gain legal acceptance.

Commodification

Earlier in this chapter, commodification was discussed in relation to cultural appropriation. Now, I discuss the role profit has on shaping Western participation in ayahuasca ceremonies, including the role of drug tourism, and the ecological toll caused by the increase in participation in ayahuasca ceremonies by Westerners, primarily Americans. There are many problems associated with the commodification of ayahuasca. One problem regarding charging high fees for ceremonies is that it can easily default into supporting a polarized classist hegemonic structure, whereby the only people who can afford to participate are a self-selecting group of primarily White, educated, middle-class people. This type of exclusivity points directly to the hegemonic structure of individuality as being the top priority, while others who are less financially successful simply cannot afford to participate. There appears to be a classist element, for instance, in those who can afford to travel to places such as Peru to participate in high-priced ayahuasca retreats. Missing from these examples of high-priced ayahuasca ceremonies and retreats is the Indigenous notion of healing as accessible to an entire community of people, which includes those who may be less wealthy, single parents living on a shoestring budget, college students who have little money, unemployed adults, and so on. It would seem that with an Indigenous model of relationality, ceremonies would be done for all and inclusion would be the priority. Some of these examples of high-priced ayahuasca ceremonies seem to go against the Indigenous model.

The popularization of ayahuasca in television shows, documentaries about DMT featured on Netflix video streaming service, magazine articles, and celebrities singing its praises have all contributed to the increase in attention about ayahuasca. The increase in attention has created new niche industries, such as drug tourism, that cater to people wanting to experience ayahuasca. Shifting the ayahuasca experience into the framework of another Western commodity means that many ayahuasca ceremony leaders, some Indigenous and some Western, now travel the United States, charging $150 to $350 per night for ayahuasca ceremonies. The average size of these groups is usually between 20 to 50 participants, although I have read stories of ayahuasca ceremonies with as many as 100 participants. However, most ayahuasca maestros in South America will only work with groups of 10 or less to ensure that each person is able to receive individual attention and healing during the ayahuasca ceremony, which calls into question the motivation for working with such large groups of people in one specific ceremony. I am certainly not suggesting that all people are using an exploitive commodification-based model for ayahuasca ceremonies usage in the United States. I have also heard several stories of people conducting ceremonies for groups of less than ten participants, and paid for on a donation basis. The people running smaller groups seem to be the exception to the rule, however. It appears that some people lead ayahuasca ceremonies for personal power and gain, which is part of the Western worldview, while others appear to be more service-based and community-oriented, which is more associated with an Indigenous worldview. There certainly are costs and risks of obtaining ayahuasca in the United States as well, and the price of obtaining ayahuasca is unknown to me. Despite the legal risks of working with and obtaining ayahuasca, the Ayahuasca Ceremony Leader suggested,

> It is worth taking the legal risks to help my relatives heal their lives and find a good way to move through the world. I give my life to the ceremonies and to this path of healing. It is crazy that government tries to mandate this sacred teacher as illegal. It shows how ignorant, misguided and sick the American legal system is, that they consider ayahuasca a drug and not a medicine.

DRUG TOURISM AND HEGEMONY

Another form the commodification of ayahuasca takes is the rise in drug tourism. Drug tourism refers to Westerners traveling to various countries in South America specifically to experience ayahuasca. With the large increase in Western people vising Peru and parts of South America to work with ayahuasca, there has been a rise in abuses and commodification, as well. The potential to profit from ayahuasca is certainly at the foundation of this increase in abuses. I am not suggesting that it is somehow negative that Western people travel to South America to work with ayahuasca; some positive things have come from drug tourism. Drug tourism has changed the way many people work with ayahuasca in South America, however, and most of the changes point to commodification and an influence of Western hegemony. Grunwell (1998) explains the Westernization of ayahuasca drug tourism: "That this industry [ayahuasca] is heavily advertised and available to anyone with financial means to undertake a trip, that it is not a hush-hush experience available only to a select few in the psychedelic drug underground, is perhaps even more astonishing" (p.

62). As a result, ayahuasca drug tourism has resulted in new industries and increased the number of people falsely claiming to be experts in leading ayahuasca ceremonies.

Ayahuasca tourism has created retreat centers that charge large sums of money for ayahuasca ceremonies. It has also resulted in crash courses in ayahuasca healing methodologies being offered to Westerners, who hope to master the art of ayahuasca healing quickly, compared to the multi-year apprenticeships Indigenous people go through to learn about leading ayahuasca ceremonies, whereby learning about ayahuasca is seen as a never ending path. For example, Blue Morpho ayahuasca retreat center located near Iquitos, Peru, charges $2,340 for a 7-day retreat, which includes 5 nights of ayahuasca ceremonies (Blue Morpho, 2015). These sorts of expensive retreat centers can be found in various locations around South America. Smaller, more remote, and, perhaps, more legitimate ayahuasca healers often charge only $75 per night of ceremony.

LACK OF ECOLOGICAL RESPECT FOR THE AYAHUASCA VINE

The ecosystems in South America are being altered by the increase in ayahuasca tourism along with the increase in demand for the ayahuasca brew, which contains the ayahuasca vine and chacruna leaves. As a result, areas where the ayahuasca vine grew freely along with the chacruna leaves may be overharvested, as Indigenous people try to make more and more ayahuasca to keep up with the demand. This tendency to clear cut and deforest for commercial interest, often by World Bank projects, Western corporations, and corrupt and misguided governments, are all examples of the hegemonic structures of anthropocentrism, whereupon the natural world is viewed simply for its commodity value, without forethought given to sustainability. Unfortunately, this potential problem is not mentioned in the popular books or television show documentaries about ayahuasca, which instead focus on the mystical healing ceremonies and the rituals, and the unusual elements of the ayahuasca ceremonies. There are multiple layers of hegemony at work here (deforestation, overharvesting of ayahuasca) all done in the name of profit. It is well documented that deforestation and destruction of the Amazon Rainforest has been happening at a rapid rate. According to Butler (2008),

Rainforests once covered 14% of the earth's land surface; now they cover a mere 6% and experts estimate that the last remaining rainforests could be consumed in less than 40 years. Experts estimate that we are losing 137 plant, animal, and insect species every single day due to rainforest deforestation. That equates to 50,000 species a year. (p. 1)

Given the increase in demand for ayahuasca, and, oftentimes, the lack of forethought and planning to protect and sustain this sacred vine and the sacred leaves by Indigenous peoples, it is possible and perhaps likely that ayahuasca may be harder to find over time. Or, it is possible that local Indigenous peoples are destroying local ecosystems designed to grow food for their villages and communities to instead grow ayahuasca. This trend towards destruction of the natural world for profit is a byproduct of Western hegemony and its belief that nature is subordinate to human beings and their needs. Hopefully other Indigenous groups and ecologically aware Westerners will focus on cultivating sustainable practices to both empower the Indigenous peoples to protect the sacred plant ayahuasca, while still ensuring that Indigenous ayahuasca ceremony leaders can support themselves financially through their work with ayahuasca.

Organizations such as the Ethnobotanical Stewardship Council (Ethnobotanical Stewardship Council, 2014) have recently emerged to focus on advocating for sustainability for plant medicines such as ayahuasca. According to their report (2014),

When used with other sustainable development approaches like sustainable tourism, carbon off-setting, sustainable forestry management, medicinal plant cultivation, and/or the development and certification of other sustainable non-timber forest products (NTFP), the planting and harvest of ayahuasca and admixture plants can compete economically and culturally with industrial development to be part of the solution to protecting the Amazon and improving the lives of Amazonian peoples (p. 10).

ABUSE OF POWER BY AYAHUASCA LEADERS

Given that ayahuasca is a powerful healing medicine, and known for its ability to alter consciousness, participants are in a vulnerable state during and after ayahuasca ceremonies, and, therefore, open to abuses from ayahuasca ceremony leaders and assistants. Grob (2005) mentions characteristics common to altered states of consciousness. Included in this list are alterations in thinking, altered time sense, perceptual alterations, and hyper-suggestibility (p. 76). When Western people work with ayahuasca in South America or in the West, they are then in a raw and vulnerable state. This vulnerability opens the door for unethical people to prey upon them. Many people report that they arrive in places such as Peru and Columbia to go on an ayahuasca retreat, only to find that the advertised prices are not available and the ceremonies actually cost more. In addition, there are other reports of ayahuasca ceremony leaders telling participants that if they do not get a large number of ayahuasca treatments, along with other shamanic treatments, they will then get sick or not heal. These types of financial exploits are one type of abuse and outside of the spirit of these healing ceremonies. These forms of abuse can be tied to Western hegemony, which pushes the idea of "survival of the fittest," whereby behavior can be justified because it enhances personal gain.

Exploitation of Women

The hierarchical, power-based, dominator model of Western hegemony is an influence in the ways in which women are exploited in ceremonies, and also point to a decline in authentic Indigenous values, whereby abuse, mistreatment of others, and manipulation are forbidden and punished. According to Hearn (2013), there are frequent reports of molestations, rapes, and negligence on behalf of supposed ayahuasca healers. This includes ayahuasca healers touching women's breasts and bodies during ayahuasca ceremonies and claiming it is part of the healing process, which points to Western hegemony playing out in terms of misogyny, and other power abuses. In my research, I have also heard stories from women who have had supposed medicine men trying to convince them to have sex, and/or being sexually harassed during ceremonies, which is far from the healing intent and ethical behavior from which most ceremony leaders operate. The dissociative states associated with the ayahuasca experience, and the Western tendency to romanticize and idolize ayahuasca leaders and the ayahuasca ceremony process, create a situation in which some unethical ayahuasca leaders prey on women. The inherent power differential between ayahuasca ceremony leader and participant, and the trust required for participants to allow themselves to be vulnerable and open during ayahuasca ceremonies requires highly ethical behavior.

Unfortunately, there appears to be a rise in women enduring various forms of abuse during ayahuasca ceremonies. Some organizations of women have formed to address issues of abuse and to find solutions to this problem. In November 2014, Annie Oak presented a lecture entitled, "Abuse of Power in Ceremonies that use Psychoactive Substances" at the Shaman Women, Plant Medicine and Psychedelics Salon hosted by the Women's Visionary Congress in Vancouver. During her speech, Oak reported,

> We have been meeting together since 2007 and we are observing a growing number of women who are coming forward to describe sexual advances by male shamans, particularly, but not limited to, ayahuasca ceremonies. We also hear from those who describe being energetically violated in different ways. As the number of people from around the world traveling to Peru, Ecuador, and other parts of Latin American to drink ayahuasca has increased, so have reports of abuses by people leading these ceremonies.

Later in her talk, Oak continued,

> First, we would like to caution those who find ayahuasca and other substances useful to be careful not to become enchanted or fall under their spell in a way that discourages critical thinking. We also see that ayahuasca ceremonies are becoming a big business and many shamans, ceremonial leaders, tour operators, owners of lodges and other parts of this industry have a vested interest in not discussing this topic, silencing those who have been violated, or somehow denigrating this discussion.

These comments by Oak are important and illustrate a real problem regarding safety for women who participate in ayahuasca ceremonies and other hallucinogens-based ceremonies.

In some extreme cases, ayahuasca healers have even ended up having participants die during their ceremonies. In August 2012, for example, 18-year-old Kyle Nolan from California paid $1,200 to attend 5 nights of ayahuasca ceremonies at the Shimbre Shamanic Center in Madre de Rios, Peru. Nolan died during his visit to the retreat center, and the ayahuasca leader Master Mancoluto buried Nolan's body on the retreat center property (Farberov, 2012). The cause of Nolan's death is still unknown.

Mancoluto, however, suggested that Nolan died during an ayahuasca ceremony, and there seems to be significant evidence to back up this claim. Death during ceremonies is extremely rare however, and this is an extreme cases of negligence by an ayahuasca healer ending in tragedy. The obvious problem is that this ayahuasca ceremony leader did not do his job, which ultimately is to protect, heal, and care for the people who come to work with him. Instead, Mancoluto was only concerned with making money and protecting himself from the negative consequences of his actions.

Psychonauts

Another problem with ayahuasca usage in the West is that a good number of ayahuasca users fall into the category of psychonauts. Psychonauts are people who experiment with hallucinogens as part of their process of self-exploration and mind expansion. This type of hallucinogen use is often recreational and not grounded within a ceremonial context. As Participant 4 of the qualitative interviews pointedly suggested, "I see a lot of Western people treat ayahuasca like LSD, and psychonauts treating it as a journey through the mind and nothing more." Instead of focusing on healing as a path, psychonauts think of hallucinogens as a way to escape from their ordinary life and be more dissociated.

Psychonauts often purchase ingredients to hallucinogenic brews such as ayahuasca or its analogs online. Analogs are plants that have similar chemical properties to other plants. In this case, some psychonauts, rather than try to make ayahuasca the way they do in South America, by combining ayahuasca vine and chacruna leaves, will look for plants that contain similar chemical compounds to these two ingredients. Or, they may synthesize DMT (the active hallucinogenic compound found in ayahuasca) from other plants in order to have a drug trip. This form of drug experimentation is part of the Western hegemonic structure that supports the belief that Western individuals should be free to do whatever they want, whenever they want, without any respect for traditions or cultural understandings of this plant teacher. This is not to suggest that all psychonauts are the same. It is not a black-and-white issue; some psychonauts are more respectful of Indigenous cultures and practices than others. Doyle (2011) discusses psychonauts in the following manner:

> Psychonauts browse the psychedelic vaults (online) to

learn about the experience of other psychonauts with different compounds, dosages, programming, and intent, and carry out their experiments accordingly. Trip reports are, then, first and foremost protocols, scripts for the better or worse, ingestion of psychedelic compounds and plants. (p. 47)

The problem with Doyle's approach is that it is situated within the Western worldview, and not the Indigenous worldview. There appears to be minimal, if any, recognition given to the plants as sentient beings. Plants are not considered teachers or healers or relatives, but simply as the means to getting high and having an unusual trip or experience. Doyle's description of psychonauts also seems to highlight the infusion of the Western worldview, which emphasizes and values logic and rationality, based on the belief that there is always an objective truth that can be reached through linear processes of discovery (Wurtz, 2005, p. 279). All of my research, however, seems to show that sacred medicine plants and plant medicine ceremonies work in a non-linear way. Furthermore, psychonauts generally apply the Western worldview to working with plant medicines, and forego the group experience to focus on themselves and their own psychic exploration. Last, psychonauts have no rigor in their supposed self-explorations. This individualistic approach risks promoting self-indulgence, spiritual tourism, and superficial understandings of plant medicines, and can drift into escapism and self-appeasment. The psychonaut approach is far from the reaches of Indigenous models for social and political change, and other elements situated within the Indigenous worldview.

The ayahuasca ceremony leader I interviewed specifically criticized psychonauts and those who attend ceremonies for what he referred to as the "wrong" reasons. He argued, "Some people attend ceremony only for the fun parts. They want to come for the rainbows and unicorns, and the pretty color show. But that's not why we come and drink ayahuasca. We come to learn how to be strong for ourselves in the face of adversity and ultimately to be strong for our friends, families and our world and become social change agents. That's what the medicine teaches us to do and empowers us to do and become." Most psychonauts are missing the healing intent and community focus that the ayahuasca ceremony can provide. Furthermore, psychonauts oftentimes misuse ayahuasca without the guidance of someone who knows what he or she is doing and is grounded in an Indigenous understanding of plant medicine ceremonies.

LACK OF POST-CEREMONY SOCIAL SUPPORT

As discussed in the Western worldview diagram, Indigenous cultures tend to be collectivist in nature. By collectivist, I am referring to having community support, including an established kinship network for emotional support, along with frequent access to community rituals and ceremonies. Ayahuasca usage in the West is often done without the support of a community and without a community context for understanding. As a result, oftentimes individuals leave ceremonies disoriented, whether in the US. or return from trips to work with ayahuasca in South America, because they are without a methodology of integration between the ayahuasca experience and their every day life. Lewis (2008), explains,

> Quite unlike shamanic initiates, Western ayahuasca users have little cultural support and guidance within which to contextualize their experiences.... Indigenous shamanic initiates, on the other hand, have the support of the master curandero (as well as their family, community, and culture at large), who helps the initiate to integrate and understand the distress that invariably results from their powerful ayahuasca experiences. (pp. 110-111).

When individuals, such as psychonauts, do not get the proper support after working with ayahuasca, and return to their normal lives, they may have spiritual crises. Individuals dealing with spiritual emergencies often seek clinical treatment for their anxiety and other distressing symptoms that happen as a result of not knowing how to integrate their normal waking life and their spiritual life. Within shamanic cultures, this sort of experience is common and understood as an initiatory experience, which is framed as a way to grow the soul and be cracked open to experience subtle spiritual influences more fully. Shamans, which in this case, include those who lead ayahuasca ceremonies, are known to straddle both the spiritual world and the every day world, and their work is to move between the two on behalf of healing people, communities, and the natural world. However, within the Western framework, this sort of experience of bridging the spiritual and material worlds may be experienced as anxiety, depression, and dissociative states of consciousness. That said, these sorts of spiritual crises may become exacerbated due to lack of social support and cultural understanding of the process (Lewis, 2008, p. 113). Some of the participants in the interviews I conducted echoed the statements that integrating ayahuasca experiences can be confusing and disorienting without social support. Participant 6, for example, stated, "After ceremony there was a sense of loneliness and isolation." Participant 1 echoed the inevitable, "The positive feelings and inspiration [post ceremony] can fade away." These examples point to a lack of social support and a lack of working within an Indigenous context as possible barriers to getting the most from the experiences. If these participants had more guidance and opportunities to process and integrate their ayahuasca experiences into their regular routines, perhaps they might gain more from the ayahuasca experiences. However, within the Western hegemonic forces of individualism and drive towards materialism, it is difficult to live in a manner that supports community participation and affords the time necessary to live relationally.

Conclusion

While there are many benefits to ayahuasca usage, along with ample evidence that it may be a potential antidote to various forms of Western hegemony, there are many challenges as well, which come down to Westerners applying their own Western worldview towards their work with ayahuasca. When applying a culturally mismatched paradigm, the results can be problematic. Various elements of cultural appropriation support the Western worldview, such as romanticizing Indigenous peoples, which keeps Westerners who work with ayahuasca stuck in the grips of Western hegemonic influences, rather than shifting way from these influences. Romanticizing, and therefore trivializing, Indigenous practices supports the Western worldview, as well.

One of the most destructive forces on Indigenous peoples and cultures are the Western hegemonic forces of commodification. Commodification has been the force behind drug tourism. The spread of ayahuasca tourist centers around South America has brought about many problems, including the exploitation of Westerners, sexual harassment, and other forms of abuse. These forms of abuse point to the movement away from traditional Indigenous values towards some of the worst elements of Western corruption, abuse of power, and exploitation of others for personal gain. Another byproduct of drug tourism is environmental destruction and the problems that go along with not employing sustainable practices to protect the sacred plants that go into making ayahuasca.

Next, psychonauts present a potentially destructive influence on ayahuasca usage in the West, because they attempt to work with ayahuasca outside of a ceremonial context, without the support of others in a spiritual community, or without a trained leader. The approach that psychonauts seem to take appears to be more about drug experimentation than working to move away from the destructive forces of Western hegemony. Furthermore, most Westerners, given that they are not Indigenous peoples, have small—if any—kinship networks developed. This points to potential problems with working with ayahuasca in that they do not have community to help provide emotional support that may be needed after working with ayahuasca. Westerners, and the manner in which they work with ayahuasca, oftentimes do so to support individualistic pursuits, not work to move towards a more relational Indigenous model. The influences of Western hegemony itself may prevent the ayahuasca experience from effectively combatting that same hegemony.

Conclusion

Let's revisit the term "ayagogy" again. I chose the term ayagogy because it frames ayahuasca and ayahuasca ceremonies as a learning and educational model. As an educator, I propose that ayahuasca ceremonies are themselves a form of adult learning, and the catalyst for learning and teaching is the plant teacher ayahuasca. Ayagogy integrates adult learning, the development of critical consciousness, Indigenous models for learning, and elements of transformational learning into its own unique method of healing and learning. I propose ayagogy as a social change model and a different view of working with plant medicines and plant teachers. This book has shown that ayahuasca is a potential antidote to Western hegemony, if done in a ceremonial context; if people attend ceremonies in a humble way, open to changing their lives, looking deeply at themselves, and honest with themselves about what works and does not work in their lives; and if they are rigorous with their own exploration of the toxic forces and influences in their lives.

I spent more than a 15 years searching to understand how Indigenous wisdom could begin to heal the damage caused by Western hegemony. Like many large problems, when I began to look at the state of the world for Indigenous people, I saw layers upon layers of exploitation and cultural destruction. And yet, I saw deep profound wisdom. I found ideas and ways of living that pulverized my own shallow ego. I found teachers who often lived with humor and in the flow with nature, more than I could find in the culture I grew up with. I went through some of the same processes many others went through, first romanticizing Indigenous wisdom, then being naively disappointed that those peoples were real. I dug deeper and saw my own humanity, my own failings, and then was able to accept others a bit more.

But then, I dug deeper. I had seen many friends transform through working with ayahuasca and other plant medicines. I had seen the foundation of beliefs shattered, and oftentimes people operating with more compassion, more awareness of themselves and also social awareness. This was not some Utopian vision I had or experienced, they were hard lessons, sobering lessons. No one walked on water. People became more "real", more "grounded", and more embracing of life and its innate ups and downs. Working with plant medicines softened me, opened my heart, made me see how inauthentically I was living, and how shallow my view of being a man was. Working with plant medicines and attending Indigenous ceremonies turned my life upside down and forced me to question my life, my values, my drive towards commodification, my own delusions around being a solitary individual in the world of sentient beings, and my own disconnection from the flow of nature.

And then, the rug was pulled out from under me again. While doing my doctoral research, after years of being confused and unclear of the manner in which hegemony works in our culture and around the world to exploit and keep people stuck in the muck of various forms of enslavement, a light went on. I had an "aha" moment in which I saw how deep this form of dominance influences nearly every single element of our world and lives. That sounds dramatic, but actually true in my view, and hopefully you see how deep Western hegemony runs from reading this book. From how I would wake up and my movement away from my own natural body rhythms to program myself to wake up to go to a job, to make money, to buy stuff, and my persistent drive to succeed. To the products I use in my house, the food I eat or not do not, the foods I crave that damage my body—like overly processed sweet foods, deep fried foods, process carbohydrates, fast food, and so on. I saw how hegemony has influenced my view of myself as a man and what that supposedly means—on a cultural and social level, and, therefore, believing what the media proposes men should be like and the corresponding view that I will never measure up unless I buy certain products or act and look particular ways. I saw how Western hegemony influences my views on sexuality, on gender, certainly my views of animals and plants and humans being on the topic of the ladder. My views of knowledge—and my own pre-programmed value that academic learning and research was somehow more legitimate than Indigenous learning and indigenous wisdom. I could keep going on and on.

I saw myself inside The Matrix. I was able to locate myself inside my preprogrammed bullshit and then saw a way out, a way to start to shed those skins and be slightly liberated from hegemony. I don't want to lie and suggest a miracle happened and suddenly the sky parted and I drank ayahuasca, and I was forever changed and I was never influenced by hegemony again. That would be ridiculous, naïve, and a fairy tale. I will say that, by looking deeply at hegemony, I saw that it may be possible to shed some of the influences and to begin to operate with more personal freedom.

The question is, so what? So what if I as an individual have more freedom and even happiness? That may be good and well, but the reason I am publishing this book, concentrating on ayagogy, and the reason I am passionate about this topic is to help others heal and be able to step away from the affects of Western hegemony. What I saw from doing my research and looking at this question internally is something that sounds almost embarrassing and naïve in the world today: the purpose of my research is to attack Western hegemony, and help others be free from its grips, too. One solution, I propose, is to move towards "relationality" as I describe in Chapter 4. Within this possible solution, individuals reposition themselves as community members—not just individuals. Another potential solution is to step away from the trappings of the American dream and become more aware and empathetic to the suffering of other sentient beings, and then to work to correct these problems. My hope is that ayagogy has inspired you on some level to fight against hegemony as well. Maybe this book may has changed your view of the power of plant medicines, not simply as a hallucinogen, but something which has the potential to be a social change agent. Maybe this book has perhaps challenged some of your own assumptions, and broadened your appreciation, not just for Indigenous wisdom, but also for ayahuasca in general.

I will continue my research on plant medicines, especially ayahuasca. My plan is to do more interviews with ceremony leaders and participants, and conduct more scaled questionnaires. I am planning to organize local-based, experiential conferences about ayahuasca and hegemony.

I would like to stay in contact with you directly. Please email me with questions or comments: rkaufman@email.fielding.edu. Please keep an eye on my website ayagogy.com

Please stay motivated to be a beacon of light in this oftentimes dark work.

References

Aguirre, A. (2014, February, 18). The new power trip: Inside the world of ayahuasca. Retrieved from http://www.marieclaire.com/world-reports/ayahuasca-new-power-trip

Aldred, L. (2000). Plastic shamans and astroturf sun dances: New age commercialization of Native American spirituality. The American Indian Quarterly, 24(3), 329-352.

Alexander, B. (2014, April 25). What is ayahuasca? Lindsay Lohan's "cleanse" is probably illegal, causes vomiting. Retrieved from http://www.today.com/health/what-ayahuasca-lindsay-lohans-cleanse-illegal-causes-vomiting-1D79574411

Alexander, R. (2004). Still no pedagogy? Principle, pragmatism and compliance in primary education. Cambridge Journal of Education, 34(1), 7-33.

Alfred, T. (1999). Peace, Power, and Righteousness: An Indigenous Manifesto. Oxford, UK: Oxford University Press.

Alston, D., & Brown, N. (1993). Global threats to people of color. In B.L. Bullard (Ed.). Confronting environmental racism: Voices from the grassroots, (pp. 179-194). Boston, MA: South End Press.

Anxiety and Depression Association of America. (2015). Retrieved from http://www.adaa.org/about-adaa/press-room/facts-statistics\

Armour-Thomas, E., & Gordon, E. W. (2012). Toward an understanding of assessment as a dynamic component of pedagogy. Unpublished manuscript.

Atkinson, J. (2002). Trauma trails, recreating song lines: The transgenerational effects of trauma in Indigenous Australia. North Melbourne, Australia: Spinifex Press.

Bain, K. (2013, November, 13). Ten celebrity ayahuasca users. Retrieved from http://www.laweekly.com/westcoastsound/2013/11/22/ten-celebrity-ayahuasca-users

Barbosa, P.C.R., Cazorla, I.M., Giglio, J.S., & Strassman, R. (2009). A six-month prospective evaluation of personality traits, psychiatric symptoms and quality of life in ayahuasca-naïve subjects. Journal of Psychoactive Drugs, 41(3), 205-212.

Barbosa, P. C. R., Mizumoto, S., Bogenschutz, M. P., & Strassman, R. J. (2012).

Health status of ayahuasca users. Drug Testing and Analysis, 4(7-8), 601-609.

Barreiro, J. (2010). Thinking in Indian: A John Mohawk reader. Golden, CO: Fulcrum.

Basso, K. H. (1996). Wisdom sits in places: Landscape and language among the Western Apache. Albuquerque: University of New Mexico Press.

Bataille, G.M. (Ed). (2001). Native American representations: First encounters, distorted images, and literary appropriations. Lincoln: University of Nebraska Press.

Battiste, M. (2005). Indigenous knowledge: Foundations for first nations. World Indigenous Nations Higher Education Consortium-WINHEC Journal.

Bell, R.G. (Producer), Fincher, D. (Director). (1999). Fight Club [Motion Picture]. USA: 20th Century Fox.

Bernd, C. (2013, January 29). Idle No More: From grassroots to global movement. Truthout. Retrieved from http://truth-out.org/news/item/14165-idle-no-more-from-grassroots-to- global-movement

Beyer, S.V. (2007, December 12). Strong sweet smells. (blog article). Retrieved from http://www.singingtotheplants.com/2007/12/strong-sweet-smells/

Beyer, S.V. (2012, April 25). On the origins of ayahuasca. (blog article). Retrieved from http://www.singingtotheplants.com/2012/04/on-origins-of-ayahuasca/

Bishop, R. (2008). Te Kotahitanga: Kaupapa Maori in mainstream classrooms. In N. Denzin, Y.S. Lincoln, & L.T. Smith (Eds.), Handbook of critical and Indigenous methodologies (pp. 439-458). Los Angeles CA: Sage.

Blaut, J.M. (1993). The colonizer's model of the world: Geographical diffusionism and Eurocentric history. New York, NY: The Guildford Press.

Blue Morpho. (2015). Retrieved from http://www.bluemorphotours.com/dates-and-prices.html

Bourdain, A. (2013). The wages of cacao. Retrieved from http://www.cnn.com/video/shows/anthony-bourdain-parts-unknown/episode7/index.html

Bouso, J. C., & Riba, J. (2014). Ayahuasca and the treatment of drug addiction. In B.C. Labate & C. Cavnar (Eds.), The Therapeutic Use of Ayahuasca (pp. 95-109). Berlin: Springer Berlin Heidelberg.

Bowers, C. A. (2000). Let them eat data: How computers affect education, cultural diversity, and the prospects of ecological sustainability. Athens: University of Georgia Press.

Bowers, C. A. (2005). Educating for a sustainable future: Mediating between the commons and economic globalization. Retrieved from http://cabowers.net/pdf/Educatingforasustainablefuture.pdf

Brierley, D. I., & Davidson, C. (2012). Developments in harmine pharmacology—Implications for ayahuasca use and drug-dependence treatment. Progress in Neuro-Psychopharmacology and Biological Psychiatry, 39(2), 263-272.

Brookfield, S.D. (1995). The getting of wisdom: What critically reflective teaching is and why it's important. In Becoming a critically reflective teacher, (pp. 1-28). San Francisco, CA: Jossey-Bass.

Brookfield, S.D. (2005). The power of critical theory: Liberating adult learning and teaching. San Francisco CA: Jossey-Bass.

Bullis, R. K. (2008). The "vine of the soul" vs. the Controlled Substances Act: implications of the hoasca case. Journal of Psychoactive Drugs, 40(2), 193-199.

Butler, R. A. (2008). Deforestation in the Amazon. Retrieved from http://www.mongabay.com/brazil.html

Cajete, G. (1994). Look to the mountain: An ecology of Indigenous education. Skyland, NC: Kivaki Press.

Cantoni, G. (2007). Stabilizing Indigenous languages. A Center for Excellence in Education Monograph. Northern Arizona University, Flagstaff.

Carragee, K. M., & Roefs, W. (2004). The neglect of power in recent frame research. Journal of Communication, 54, 214-233.

Castellano, M. B. (2000). Updating Aboriginal traditions of knowledge. In G. J. S. Dei, B. L. Hall, & D. G. Rosenburg (Eds.), Indigenous knowledges in global contexts (pp. 21-36). Toronto, Ontario, Canada: University of Toronto Press.

Castellano, M.B. (2004, January). Ethics of Aboriginal research. Journal of Aboriginal Health, 1(1), 98-114.

Charing, H. G., Cloudsley, P.E., Amaringo, P. (2011). The ayahuasca visions of Pablo Amaringo. Rochester, VT: Inner Traditions.

Church, J.A. (2014, March 17). The evidence shows sea levels are rising: Let's not be caught out. ECOS, No. 193.

Churchill, W. (2002). Struggle for the land: Native North American resistance to genocide. San Francisco, CA: City Lights Books.

Clements, E. (2004). The limits of self-determination. Convergence, Volume XXXVI1, (2), 65-77.

Cohen, A. (2014, April 21). My journey with a life altering drug: Ayahuasca. Retrieved from http://www.elle.com/beauty/health-fitness/ayahuasca-drug

Controlled Substance Act (CSA). 2000. 84 Stat. 1242 as amended 21 U.S.C. §§ 801-904 (2000 ed. and Supp. 1).

David, P. A. (2003). Koyaanisqatsi in cyberspace. Stanford Institute for Economic Policy Research (SIEPR), Discussion Paper, 02-29.

Davidson, D. (2014, April 14). No let-up by Sarawak natives who continue to obstruct dam. The Malaysian Insider, Retrieved from http://www.themalaysianinsider.com/malaysia/article/no-let-up-by-sarawak-natives-who- continue-to-obstruct-dam

Dei, S.G., Hall, B.L., & Rosenberg, D.G. (2000). Situating Indigenous knowledges: Definitions and boundaries. In S.G. Dei, B.L. Hall, & D.G. Rosenberg (Eds.), Indigenous knowledges in global contexts: Multiple readings of our world (pp. 3-20). Toronto, ON: University of Toronto Press.

Deloria, V. (1973). God is red. New York, NY: Grosset & Dunlap.

Deloria, V., & Lytle, C. M. (1983). American Indians, American justice. Austin: University of Texas Press.

Deloria, V., & Wildcat, D. (2001). Power and place. Golden, CO: Fulcrum Resources.

Derber, C. (1979). The pursuit of attention: Power and individualism in everyday life. New York, NY: Oxford University Press.

De Rios, M. D. (1984). Visionary vine: Hallucinogenic healing in the Peruvian Amazon. Long Grove, IL: Waveland Press.

De Rios, M. D. (1996). On "Human Pharmacology of Hoasca": A medical anthropology perspective. The Journal of Nervous and Mental Disease, 184(2), 95-98.

De Rios, M. D., & Rumrrill, R. (2008). A hallucinogenic tea, laced with controversy: Ayahuasca in the Amazon and the United States. Westport, CT: Praeger.

de Shazer, S. (1985). Keys to solution in brief therapy. New York, NY: Norton.

Dombeck, M. (2007, January 20). Robert Kegan's awesome theory on social maturity (Blog post). Retrieved from http://www.mentalhelp.net/poc/view_doc.php?type=doc&id=11433

Doyle, R. M. (2011). Darwin's pharmacy: Sex, plants, and the evolution of the noösphere. Seattle: University of Washington Press.

Dunn, J. (1998, February 5). Sting. Rolling Stone Magazine.

Dyson, L.E., & Underwood, J. (2006, April). Indigenous people on the web. Journal of Theoretical and Applied Electronic Commerce Research, 1, 65-76.

Ebenstein, A. (2012). The consequences of industrialization: Evidence from water pollution and digestive cancers in China. Review of Economics and Statistics, 94(1), 186-201.

Eckersley, R. (2006). Is modern Western culture a health hazard? International Journal of Epidemiology, 35(2), 252-258.

Eduardo, L., Luna, L. E., & Amaringo, P. (1999). Ayahuasca visions: The religious iconography of a Peruvian shaman. Berkeley, CA: North Atlantic Books.

Erikson, E. (1963). Childhood and society. New York, NY: Norton.

Ermine, W., Sinclair, R., & Jeffrey, B. (2004). The ethics of research involving Indigenous peoples. Saskatoon, SK: Indigenous Peoples' Health Research Centre.

Eshowsky, M. (1999, Winter/Spring). Shamanism and peacemaking. Shamanism, 12(2), 4-9.

Ethnobotanical Stewardship Council. (2014, November). The ayahuasca dialogues report: Preliminary research and prospects for safer and more sustainable ayahuasca.

Fanon, F. (1994). On national culture. In P. Williams & L. Chrisman (Eds.), Colonial discourse and post colonial theory (pp 36-52). New York, NY: Columbia University Press.

Farberov, S. (2012, September 12). Peruvian shaman confesses he buried body of U.S. teen who died from drinking hallucinogenic herbal brew at spiritual retreat. The Daily Mall.com Retrieved from http://www.dailymail.co.uk/news/article-2202459/Kyle-Joseph-Nolan-death-Peruvian-shaman-confesses-buried-body-U-S-teen-spiritual-retreat.html#ixzz3PtTIFs4U

Farr, A. L. (2009). Critical theory and democratic vision: Herbert Marcuse and recent liberation philosophies. Lanham, MD: Lexington Books.

Fecteau, L. M. (2001). Ayahuasca patent revocation: Raising questions about current US. patent policy. Boston College Third World Law Journal, 21(1), 69-104.

Fletcher, M. L. (2004). Theoretical restrictions on the sharing of Indigenous biological knowledge: Implications for freedom of speech in tribal law. Kan. JL & Pub. Pol'y, 14, 525.

Foucault, M. (1980). Power/knowledge: Selected interviews and other writings, 1972-1977. New York, NY: Pantheon.

Four Arrows. (2006). Unlearning the language of conquest: Scholars expose anti-Indianism in America. Austin: University of Texas Press.

Four Arrows. (2010, April). Wolokokiapia: An antidote to neo-liberalism's influence on war and peace. Peace Studies Journal, 3(1).

Four Arrows & Narvaez, D. (2014). A more authentic baseline. (unpublished paper).

Frecska, E., White, K. D., & Luna, L. E. (2003). Effects of the Amazonian psychoactive beverage ayahuasca on binocular rivalry: Interhemispheric switching or interhemispheric fusion? Journal of Psychoactive Drugs, 35(3), 367-374.

Freedland, C. S., & Mansbach, R. S. (1999). Behavioral profile of constituents in ayahuasca, an Amazonian psychoactive plant mixture. Drug and alcohol dependence, 54(3), 183-194.

Freire, P. (2004). Pedagogy of the oppressed: 30th Anniversary Edition. New York, NY: Continuum.

Gile, A. (2008). Ayahuasca cosmology. Unpublished manuscript.

Gilligan, C. (1982). In a different voice. Boston, MA: Harvard University Press.

Giroux, H.A., & Giroux, S.S. (2008). Challenging neoliberalism's new world order. In N.K. Denzin, Y.S. Lincoln & L.T. Smith (Eds), Handbook of critical and Indigenous methodologies (pp. 181-190). Los Angeles, CA: Sage.

Godfrey, W. (2014, June 27). How CNN's Amber Lyon became an evangelist for psychedelic healing. Retrieved from http://www.substance.com/how-cnns-amber-lyon-became-an-evangelist-for-psychedelic healing/8138/?utm_content=buffer1cc84&utm_medium=social&utm_source=facebook.c om&utm_campaign=buffer

Gordon, U. (2009). Anarchism and the politics of technology. WorkingUSA, 12(3), 489-503.

Gramsci, A. (1971). Selections from the Prison Notebooks. (Q. Hoare & G. Nowell-Smith, Ed. & Trans.). London, UK: Lawrence and Wishart.

Grande, S. (2008). Red pedagogy: The un-methodology. In N.K. Denzin, Y.S. Lincoln, & L.T. Smith (Eds.), Handbook of critical and indigenous methodologies (pp. 85-101). Los Angeles, CA: Sage.

Grob, C. S. (2005). The psychology of ayahuasca. In R. Metzner, Sacred vine of spirits: Ayahuasca (pp. 63-93). Rochester, VT: Park Street Press.

Grob, C. S., McKenna, D. J., Callaway, J. C., Brito, G. S., Neves, E. S., Oberlaender, G., Boone, K. B. (1996). Human psychopharmacology of hoasca, a plant hallucinogen used in ritual context in Brazil. The Journal of Nervous and Mental Disease, 184(2), 86-94.

Grunwell, J.N. (1998). Ayahuasca tourism in South America. MAPS, VIII(3).

Hall, S. (1992). The West and the rest: Discourse and power. In S. Hall & B. Gielben (Eds.), Formation of modernity (pp. 276-320). Cambridge, UK: Polarity Press & Open University.

Harjo, J., & Bird, G. (1997). Introduction. In Reinventing the enemy's language (pp. 19-21). New York, NY: W. W. Norton.

Harkness, S., Super, C. M., & Tijen, N. V. (2000). Individualism and the "Western mind" reconsidered: American and Dutch parents' ethnotheories of the child. New Directions for Child and Adolescent Development, 87, 23-39.

Harms, J., & Kellner, D. (1991). Toward a critical theory of advertising. Current Perspectives in Social Theory, 11, 41-67.

Harris, R., & Gurel, L. (2012). A study of ayahuasca use in North America. Journal of Psychoactive Drugs, 44(3), 209-215.

Hearn, K. (2013, March). The dark side of ayahuasca. Men's Journal. Retrieved from http://www.mensjournal.com/magazine/the-dark-side-of-ayahuasca-20130215

Heaven, R., & Charing, H. G. (2006). Plant spirit shamanism: Traditional techniques for healing the soul. Rochester, VT: Inner Traditions/Bear.

Hedlund-de Witt, A. (2013). Worldviews and their significance for the global sustainable development debate: A philosophical exploration of the evolution of a concept. Environmental Ethics, 35.

Herman, E. S., & Chomsky, N. (2008). Manufacturing consent: The political economy of the mass media. New York, NY: Random House.

Hofstede, G. (2011). Dimensionalizing cultures: The Hofstede model in context. Online Readings in Psychology and Culture, 2(1), 8.

hooks, B. (2003). Teaching community: A pedagogy of hope (Vol. 36). New York, NY: Routledge.

Humphreys, D. (1996). Hegemonic ideology and the international tropical timber organization. In J. Vogler & M. Imber (Eds.), The Environment and International Relations, (pp. 215-233). London, UK: Routledge.

Huntington, S. P. (1996). The West: Unique, not universal. Foreign Affairs, 28-46.

Ibrahim, F. A. (1991). Contribution of cultural worldview to generic counseling and development. Journal of Counseling & Development, 70(1), 13-19.

Idle No More. (2013). Official site: http://idlenomore.ca

Iseke, J. (2013, Winter). Indigenous storytelling as research. International Review of Qualitative Research, 6(4) 559-577.

Jacobs, D.T. (1998). Primal awareness. Rochester, VT: Inner Traditions.

Jacobs, D.T. (2013). Teaching truly: A curriculum to indigenize mainstream education. New York NY: Peter Lang.

Jiang, Z. (2011). A research and counter-measures of English cultural hegemony in China. Asian Social Science, 7(1).

Jowitt, J. (2010, February 18). World's top firms cause $2.2tn of environmental damage, report estimates. The Guardian, Environmental section.

Jung. C.G. (1981). The development of personality. Princeton, NJ: Princeton University Press.

Kaituhi, T. (2013, November 25). West Coast Maori protest against Anadarko oil drilling. IC magazine. Retrieved from http://intercontinentalcry.org/west-coast-maori-protest-against-anadarko-oil-drilling-21199/

Katz, H. (2006). Gramsci, hegemony, and global civil society networks. Voluntas: International Journal of Voluntary and Nonprofit Organizations, 17(4), 332-347.

Kegan, R. (1992). The evolving self. Cambridge, MA: Harvard University Press.

Khadem, S.J. (2008). Medicine Path: Spiritualist and new age representations of

Native Americans (Doctoral dissertation, New School for Social Research, 2008). ProQuest dissertations and Theses: 2009.

Kimberling, J. (2005). Indigenous Peoples and the oil frontier in Amazonia: The case of Ecuador, ChevronTexaco, and Aguinda v. Texaco. NYUJ Int'l. L. & Pol., 38, 413.

Kincheloe, J.L., & Steinberg, S.R. (2008). Indigenous knowledges in education: Complexities, dangers, and profound benefits. In N.K. Denzin, Y.S. Lincoln, & L.T. Smith (Eds.), Handbook of critical and Indigenous methodologies (pp. 135-156). Los Angeles, CA: Sage.

Kivel, P. (2013). Living in the shadow of the cross: Understanding and resisting the power and privilege of Christian hegemony. Gabriola Island, Canada: New Society.

Kjellgren, A., Eriksson, A., & Norlander, T. (2009). Experiences of encounters with ayahuasca—"the vine of the soul". Journal of Psychoactive Drugs, 41(4), 309-315.

Knowles, M. S. (1970). The modern practice of adult education (Vol. 41). New York: New York Association Press.

Knowles, M. S. (1980). The modern practice of adult education. New York: Cambridge, The Adult Education Company.

Kovach, M. E. (2009). Indigenous methodologies: Characteristics, conversations, and contexts. Toronto, ON: University of Toronto Press.

Labate, B. C., & Cavnar, C. (Eds.). (2013). The therapeutic use of ayahuasca. Berlin, Germany: Springer Berlin.

Labate, B. C., MacRae, E., & Goulart, S. L. (2010). Brazilian ayahuasca religions in perspective. In B.C. Labate, E. MacRae (Eds.). Ayahuasca, ritual and religion in Brazil, (pp. 1-20). London, UK: Equinox.

Labate, B.C., De Rose, I.S., & dos Santos, R.G. (2008). Ayahuasca religions: A comprehensive bibliography and critical essays. MAPS (Multidisciplinary Associated for Psychedelic Studies).

Ladson-Billings, G. (2003). Racialized discourse and ethnic epistemologies. In N. Denzin & S. Lincoln (Eds.), The landscape of qualitative research (pp. 398-433). Thousand Oaks, CA: Sage.

LaDuke, W. (1999). All our relations: Native struggles for land and life. Cambridge, MA: South End Press.

Lewis, S. E. (2008). Ayahuasca and spiritual crisis: Liminality as space for personal growth. Anthropology of Consciousness, 19(2), 109-133.

Little, S., Holmes L., & Grieco, M. (2001). Calling up culture: Information spaces and

information flows as the virtual dynamics of inclusion and exclusion. Information Technology & People. 14(4), 353-367.

Luna, L. E. (2011). Indigenous and mestizo use of ayahuasca: An overview. In R.G. Santos (Ed.), The ethnopharmacology of ayahuasca, (pp. 1-21). Kerala, India: Transworld Research Network.

Mabit, J. (2007). Ayahuasca in the treatment of addictions. Psychedelic Medicine: New Evidence for Hallucinogenic Substances as Treatments, 2, 87-105.

Maroukis, T. C. (2012). The peyote road: Religious freedom and the Native American Church (Vol. 265). Norman: University of Oklahoma Press.

Martin, G. J. (2010). Ethnobotany: A methods manual. New York, NY: Routledge.

Master, P. (1998). Positive and negative aspects of the dominance of English. TESOL Quarterly, 32(4), 716-727.

Mate, G. (2013, May 30). Healing trauma with ayahuasca. Retrieved from http://larahentz.wordpress.com/2013/06/01/healing-trauma-with-ayahuasca-dr-gabor-mate/

Maurial, M. (1999). Indigenous knowledge and schooling: A continuum between conflict and dialogue. In L. M. Semali & J. L. Kincheloe (Eds.), What is Indigenous knowledge: Voices from the academy (pp. 59-77). New York, NY: Falmer Press.

McIntosh, P. (1989). White privilege: Unpacking the invisible knapsack. Peace and Freedom, 49(4), 10-12.

McKenna, D. J. (1998). Ayahuasca: An ethnopharmacologic history. In R. Metzner, Sacred vine of spirits: Ayahuasca (pp. 40-62). Rochester, VT: Park Street Press.

McKenna, D. J. (2004). Clinical investigations of the therapeutic potential of ayahuasca:Rationale and regulatory challenges. Pharmacology & Therapeutics, 102, 111–129.

McLoughlin, C. (1999). Culturally responsive technology use: Developing an on-line community of learners. British Journal of Educational Technology. 30(3), 231–243.

Memmi, A. (2000). Racism. Minneapolis: University of Minnesota Press.

Mercer, J., Kelman, I., Taranis, L., & Suchet-Pearson, S. (2009). Framework for integrating Indigenous and scientific knowledge for disaster risk reduction. Disasters, 34, 214–239.

Metzner, R. (Ed.). (2005). Sacred vine of spirits: Ayahuasca. Rochester, VT: Inner Traditions/Bear.

Mezey, N. (2007). The paradoxes of cultural property. Columbia Law Review, 107, 2004-2046.

Mezirow, J. (1981). A critical theory of adult learning and education. Adult Education Quarterly, 32(1), 3-24.

Mezirow, J. (1996). Contemporary paradigms of learning. Adult Education Quarterly, 46, 158– 172.

Mihesuah, D.A. (1996). American Indians: Stereotypes and realities. Atlanta, GA: Clarity Press.

Mihesuah, D.A. (2003). Indigenous American women: Decolonization, empowerment, activism. Lincoln: University of Nebraska Press.

Miller, L. S. (1984). United States Patent No. PP5, 751, United States Patent Office.

Mizrach, S. (2003). Ayahuasca, shamanism, and curanderismo in the Andes. Retrieved from http://www2.fiu.edu/~mizrachs/yage.html

Morris, B. (2014, June 13). Ayahuasca: A strong cup of tea. Retrieved from http://www.nytimes.com/2014/06/15/fashion/ayahuasca-a-strong-cup-of-tea.html?_r=1

Nakata, M. (1998). Anthropological texts and Indigenous standpoints. Australian Aboriginal Studies. (2), 3-12.

Native Action Org. (2012). Retrieved from http://www.nativeaction.org/staff.html

Native Women's Association of Canada (NWAC). (2003). Our way of being: Gathering of Indigenous women on self-government. A NWAC Position paper. Retrieved from http://www.nwac.ca/sites/default/files/reports/OurWayofBeing.pdf

Newman, M. (1994). Defining the enemy: Adult education in social action. Sydney, Australia: Stewart Victor.

Nielson, J. L., & Megler, J. D. (2014). Ayahuasca as a candidate therapy for PTSD. In B.C. Labate & C. Cavnar (Eds.). The therapeutic use of ayahuasca (pp. 41-58). Germany: Springer Berlin Heidelberg.

Oak, A. (2014, December 30). Abuse of power in ceremonies that use psychoactive substances. Women's Visionary Congress. Retrieved from http://visionarycongress.org/abuse-of-power-in-ceremonies-that-use-psychoactive-substances/

Okazaki, S., David, E. J. R., & Abelmann, N. (2008). Colonialism and psychology of culture. Social and Personality Psychology Compass, 2(1), 90-106.

Omi, M., & Winant, H. (1994). Racial formation in the United States. New York, NY: Routledge.

Orbach, S. (1986). Hunger strike: The anorectic's struggle as a metaphor for our age. New York, NY: Avon.

O'Sullivan, E. (2003). Bringing a perspective of transformative learning to globalized consumption. International Journal of Consumer Studies, 27 (4), 326–330.

Persaud, R. B. (2001). Counter-hegemony and foreign policy: The dialectics of marginalized and global forces in Jamaica. Albany: SUNY Press.

Peters, J., & Wolper, A. (Eds.). (1995). Women's rights, human rights: International feminist perspectives. New York, NY: Psychology Press.

Proctor, R. (2001). Tourism opens new Doors, creates New challenges, for traditional healers in Peru. Cultural Survival Quarterly, 24(4), 14-16.

Puchala, D. J. (2005). World hegemony and the United Nations. International Studies Review, 7(4), 571-584.

Riba, J., Valle, M., Urbano, G., Yritia, M., Morte, A., & Barbanoj, M. J. (2003). Human pharmacology of ayahuasca: Subjective and cardiovascular effects, monoamine metabolite excretion, and pharmacokinetics. Journal of Pharmacology and Experimental Therapeutics, 306(1), 73-83.

Rich, A. (1982). On lies, secrets, and silence. New York, NY: W.W. Norton Company.

Rising, M., & Dougall, M. (2013, August 29). Sweden's Indigenous Sami in fight against miners. AP.org. Retrieved from http://bigstory.ap.org/article/swedens-indigenous-sami-fight-against-miners

Rivier, L., & Lindgren, J. E. (1972). "Ayahuasca," the South American hallucinogenic drink: An ethnobotanical and chemical investigation. Economic Botany, 26(2), 101.

Robinson, W. I. (2005). Gramsci and globalisation: From nation?state to transnational hegemony. Critical Review of International Social and Political Philosophy, 8(4), 559-574.

Rogers, R.A. (2006). From cultural exchange to transculturation: A review and reconceptualization of cultural appropriation. Communication Theory, 16, 474-503.

Sahtouris, E. (1989). Gaia: The human journey from chaos to cosmos. New York, NY: Pocket Books.

Schnarch, B. (2004). Ownership, control, access, and possession (OCAP) or self-determination applied to research. Journal of Aboriginal Health, 1(1), 80-95.

Schubert, L., Dye, T., & Zeigler, H. (2015). The irony of democracy: An uncommon introduction to American politics. Boston, MA: Cengage Learning.

Schultes, R. E. (1982). The beta-carboline hallucinogens of South America. Journal of Psychoactive Drugs, 14(3), 205-220.

Semali, L. (1999a). Community as classroom: Dilemmas of valuing African indigenous literacy in education. International Review of Education, 45(¾), 305-319.

Semali, L. (1999b). What is Indigenous knowledge?: Voices from the academy. New York, NY: Routledge.

Shandrow, K.L. (2014, September 18). What does Mark Cuban do first thing in the morning? Entrepreneur. Retrieved from http://www.entrepreneur.com/article/237616

Shanon, B. (2002). The antipodes of the mind: Charting the phenomenology of the ayahuasca experience. New York, NY: Oxford University Press.

Sheehy, J. F. (1999). The Church's history of injustice and why this priest left. Lanham, MD: University Press of America.

Shor, I. (1992). Empowering education. Chicago, IL: The University of Chicago Press.

Shor, I. (1993). Education in politics: Paulo Freire's critical pedagogy. In P. Leonard, & P. McLaren (Eds.), Paulo Freire: A critical encounter (pp. 24-35). New York, NY: Routledge.

Simpson, L. (2000). Anishinaabe ways of knowing. In J. Oakes, R. Riew, S. Koolage, L. Simpson, & N. Schuster (Eds.), Aboriginal health, identity and resources (pp. 165-185). Winnipeg, Manitoba, Canada: Native Studies Press.

Smith, L.T. (1999). Decolonizing methodologies: Research and Indigenous peoples. New York, NY: St. Zed Books.

Sobiecki, J. F. (2013). An account of healing depression using ayahuasca plant teacher medicine in a Santo Daime ritual. Indo-Pacific Journal of Phenomenology, 13(1), 1-10.

Strassman, R. (2001). DMT: The spirit molecule. Rochester, VT: Park Street Press.

Sue, D.W. (1978). World views and counseling. The Personnel and Guidance Journal, 56, 583-592.

Tarnas, R. (2006). Cosmos and psyche: Intimations of a new world view. New York: Viking.

Temple of the Way of Light. (2015). Retrieved from http://templeofthewayoflight.org/shamanism-ayahuasca/respecting-tradition/

Thomas, G., Lucas, P., Capler, N. R., Tupper, K. W., & Martin, G. (2013). Ayahuasca-assisted therapy for addiction: Results from a preliminary observational study in Canada. Current Drug Abuse Reviews, 6(1), 30-42.

Topping, D.M. (1998). Ayahuasca and cancer: One man's experience. Bulletin of the Multidisciplinary Association for Psychedelic Studies, 8(3), 22–26.

Tupper, K. W. (2002). Entheogens and existential intelligence: The use of plant teachers as cognitive tools. Canadian Journal of Education, 27, 499–516.

Tupper, K.W. (2008). The globalization of ayahuasca: Harm reduction or benefit maximization? International Journal of Drug Policy, 19, 297–303.

Tupper, K. W. (2009a). Ayahuasca healing beyond the Amazon: The globalization of a traditional Indigenous entheogenic practice. Global Networks, 9(1), 117-136.

Tupper, K. W. (2009b). Entheogenic healing: The spiritual effects and therapeutic potential of ceremonial ayahuasca use. In J. H. Ellens (Ed.), The healing power of spirituality: How faith helps humans thrive (Vol. 3, pp. 269-282). Westport, CT: Praeger.

Tupper, K. W. (2011). Ayahuasca in Canada: Cultural phenomenon and policy issue. The internationalization ayahuasca. Göttingen: Hofgrefe.

Ulloa, A. (2013). The ecological native: Indigenous peoples' movements and eco-governmentality in Columbia. New York, NY: Routledge.

Vidal, J. (2011, April 10). Bolivia enshrines natural world's rights with equal status for Mother Earth. The Guardian. Retrieved from http://www.guardian.co.uk/environment/2011/apr/10/bolivia-enshrines-natural-worlds-rights

Welton, M. (1995). In defense of the lifeworld. Albany: State University of New York.

West, C. (1982). Prophesy deliverance: An Afro-American revolutionary Christianity. Philadelphia, PA: Westminster Press.

Wheatley, M.J. (1999). Leadership and the new science. San Francisco CA: Berret-Koehler Publishers.

Wilson, S. (2008). Research is ceremony: Indigenous research methods. Winnipeg, Manitoba Fernwood.

Winkelman, M. (2005). Drug tourism or spiritual healing? Ayahuasca seekers in Amazonia. Journal of Psychoactive Drugs, 37(2), 209-218.

Winkelman, M. (2014). Therapeutic applications of ayahuasca and other sacred medicines. In B.C. Labate & C. Cavnar (Eds.), The Therapeutic Use of Ayahuasca (pp. 1-21). Berlin, Germany: Springer Berlin Heidelberg.

Winkelman, M., & Roberts, T. B. (2007). Psychedelic medicine: New evidence for hallucinogenic substances as treatments (2 volumes). Westport, CT: Greenwood.

Wolf, N. (2002). The beauty myth: How images of beauty are used against women. New York, NY: Perennial.

Wurtz, E. (2005). Intercultural communication on web sites: A cross-cultural analysis of web sites from high-context cultures and low-context cultures. Journal of Computer-Mediated Communication, 11, 274–299. DOI: 10.1111/j.1083-6101.2006.tb00313.x

Yellow Bird, M. (2005). Beginning decolonization. In W.A. Wilson & M.A. Yellow Bird, (Eds.), For Indigenous eyes only: A decolonization handbook (pp. 1-7). Sante Fe, NM: School of American Research.

Zaitchik, A. (2013, March). Ayahuasca at home: An American experience. Retrieved from http://www.mensjournal.com/magazine/ayahuasca-at-home-an-american-experience- 20130215 20